TORCH BIBLE COMMENTARIES

General Editors

John Marsh and Alan Richardson

FOREWORD TO SERIES

The aim of this series of commentaries on books of the Bible is to provide the general reader with the soundest possible assistance in understanding the message of each book considered as a whole and as a part of the Bible.

The findings and views of modern critical scholarship on the text of the Bible have been taken fully into account; but we have asked the writers to remember that the Bible is more than a quarry for the practice of erudition; that it contains the message of the living God.

We hope that intelligent people of varying interests will find that these commentaries, while not ignoring the surface difficulties, are able to concentrate the mind on the essential gospel contained in the various books of the Bible.

THE GOSPEL ACCORDING TO

SAINT JOHN

The Meaning of the History of Jesus

ALAN RICHARDSON
D.D. (Oxon.), Hon. D.D. (Glasgow)
Dean of York

SCM PRESS LTD

334 00808 5

First published 1959
Second impression 1960
Third impression 1965
Fourth impression 1968
Fifth impression 1971

© *SCM Press Ltd 1959*

Printed in Great Britain by
Fletcher & Son Ltd, Norwich

CONTENTS

INTRODUCTION

COMMENTARY

I

II

III

XII

XIII

XIV

XV

XVI

XVII

XVIII

XIX

XX

XXI

INTRODUCTION

INTRODUCTION

THE JOHANNINE LITERATURE

The Johannine literature in the New Testament consists of five books: the Gospel according to St John, the three General Epistles of John, and the Revelation of St John the Divine. These works are all related to one another in some way. The Epistles are written by the author of the Gospel, or (in the opinion of some scholars) by a close disciple of his. The problem of the relation of these four works to the Book of Revelation is very complicated: the style is utterly different, but there is a surprising number of real affinities of thought and outlook, and even of vocabulary. Many of these affinities are pointed out in the Commentary. They are frequently overlooked by those who suppose that the Gospel was written by a Greek-minded Christian (even if he was himself a Jew of Palestine by birth and upbringing) for the intelligentsia of the Hellenistic world. The word 'Hellenistic' refers to that world of Greek culture—of philosophy, art, religion, gymnastics, the theatre, medicine, and so on—which had spread far beyond the frontiers of Greece and embraced virtually the whole civilization of the Mediterranean; it was the world whose *lingua franca* was Greek (the *koinē*, or common tongue), though its government was for the most part Roman. Thus, we speak of Philo of Alexandria (*c.* 20 BC—*c.* AD 50) as a Hellenistic Jew, because he combined reverence for the Law of Moses with a profound knowledge of Plato and the Greek philosophers; or we speak of Hellenistic religions (such as the Mysteries), although by origin they were oriental rather than Greek, because by the beginning of our era they had become the characteristic forms of religious observance—the 'evangelical nonconformity' of the ancient world, as over against the State worship of the classical Olympian deities, now observed only on ceremonial occasions. Recent scholarship has shewn that there had been a real flowing together of Hellenistic and Hebraic elements even in such Greek philosophies as Stoicism on the one hand or in such Hebraic systems as Palestinian rabbinic Judaism on the other. It should therefore not surprise us to find that in the Johannine literature also there is a living synthesis of Hellenistic and Hebraic elements. A problem which engages the attention of scholars to-day is the relation of these elements to each other, or the preponderance of the one over the other. It is a very complicated question, and one which we cannot discuss at length; it may perhaps suffice to remark here that a solution favoured by many scholars only a decade or two ago is now being called in question from different standpoints, the solution, namely, that the Fourth Gospel is preponderantly Hellenistic in character and purpose while the Revelation is patently Hebraic. To-day it can be seriously maintained that the author of Revelation is none other than the Evangelist himself, adopting the conventional style and imagery of current Jewish apocalyptic literature as the vehicle of the communication of his 'prophecy' to a persecuted Church. We cannot attempt the solution of such complex problems as these in so brief a Commentary as this, but we shall call attention to passages which are of special importance in the discussion of them. We shall simply assume without further argument that there is a common mind behind the Johannine literature, which may for convenience be referred to as 'St John'; but we start with no assumptions about whether it was that of an individual (the son of Zebedee; the Elder of Ephesus; the Seer of Patmos, etc.) or a whole school of teachers which flourished at the end of the apostolic age.

THE 'PROBLEM' OF THE FOURTH EVANGELIST

As we shall see below, the external evidence concerning the origin and authorship of the Fourth Gospel is too scanty and too ambiguous to establish any positive conclusions. We are therefore forced to rely upon such internal evidence as the Gospel itself provides. But here again we are met with ambiguity and reticence. It seems as if the writer of the Gospel has deliberately tried to hide his identity from us; his aim is like that which he attributes to John the Baptist, namely, to point away from himself towards Christ. Whether intentionally or not, he has covered up his tracks very well. The 'Beloved Disciple' who reclined on Jesus's bosom at the Last Supper (John 13.23; cf. 19.26; 20.2; 21.7, 20) is never named in the Gospel; it seems to be asserted in 21.24 that he was the writer of the book. If he is the same person as the 'other disciple' who secured St Peter's admission into the courtyard of the high priest's house at the trial of Jesus (18.15 f.), he must fairly certainly have been a Jew of Jerusalem, probably related by birth to the great high priestly families. (See the notes in the Commentary on the passages mentioned.) This might help to explain why the Fourth Evangelist looks at the Gospel story entirely from the point of view of Jerusalem, not from that of the Galilean disciples. The identification of the Beloved Disciple with John the Apostle, the son of Zebedee and brother of James, cannot be traced to a period earlier than the latter half of the second century AD (see below). The Epistles—at any rate the Second and Third—are simply stated to be from 'the Elder', who is not named and who does not claim to be an apostle (II John 1 and III John 1). The only place in the Johannine literature where the name 'John' is found is the Book of Revelation (Rev. 1.1, 4, 9), and here the writer speaks of himself as a

Christian prophet but does not claim to be an apostle. Indeed, he refers to 'the twelve apostles of the Lamb' in the third person, as though they were historical rather than contemporary figures (Rev. 21.14). Whether the Jerusalem disciple became later in life the 'Elder' who exercised a kind of metropolitan authority amongst the churches of some region (cf. esp. III John 9 f.); whether this region was the parts of Asia Minor around Ephesus; whether he had at some time been sent to the convict settlement on the isle of Patmos (Rev. 1.9); whether he had at any time had a special relation to John the son of Zebedee; whether in in fact he actually was the aged son of Zebedee—these are questions to which we do not know the answers. Since the evidence it too slight to establish any probability, there is little point in making a guess.

JOHN THE APOSTLE

The evidence, such as it is, does not exclude the possibility that the tradition which connects the Fourth Gospel with the name of John the son of Zebedee may be right after all. The author *might* have been a disciple of the Apostle, and this may account for the veiled claims of eye-witness authority (John 1.14; 21.24; I John 1.1-3). It is not impossible that an eye-witness of the crucifixion of Jesus should have survived until the reign of Trajan; such a one might have written his book a decade or two before his death. A theory that the Gospel was written by an eye-witness would, however, encounter two main difficulties. First, it would have to explain why an eye-witness should have had to rely so heavily upon the traditional (i.e. Synoptic) material: we shall notice in the Commentary that the evidence for the view that the Fourth Evangelist possessed a source of genuine historical information other than the Synoptic tradition is not very strong. (Even so, such considerations would not rule out the possibility that the Gospel was written by a non-Galilean disciple who had been an eye-witness only of events in Jerusalem.) Secondly, there remains the fact of the strange absence of any reference in extant Christian sources before the later decades of the second century AD to the existence of a Gospel known to have been written by an apostle or an original eye-witness of the events which he records.

A third consideration may be mentioned at this point, namely, the possibility—it is no more than that—that John the son of Zebedee was martyred at an early date, as was his brother James (Acts 12.2). As with every other aspect of this baffling problem the evidence is inconclusive. Two late writers (of the fifth and ninth centuries respectively) say that Papias (*c.* AD 140) wrote in a passage of his work now lost to us that both the brothers James and John were killed by the Jews. Against this it may be argued that Irenaeus and Eusebius (see below), who had read Papias at first hand, both held that the Apostle John survived until the closing years of the first century. More important is the question concerning Mark 10.39, in which Jesus seems to prophesy that James and John would be martyred: did St Mark know that already by the time he was writing this prophecy had been fulfilled in respect of John as it had been in respect of James? Again we must admit that we do not know.

The last that we hear of John the Apostle in the Book of Acts is his visit together with St Peter to Samaria after the success of Philip's evangelistic work there (Acts 8.14); it does not seem at all likely that St Luke knew anything about his being martyred. From St Paul we learn that John was a 'pillar' of the church in Jerusalem fourteen years after Paul's conversion (Gal. 2.1, 9). This would take us down to about the reign of Herod Agrippa I (died AD 44; cf. Acts 12.23), who killed the Apostle James. At this point all the evidence tantalizingly vanishes and the Apostle disappears into the shadows. All that we can say with certainty is that more than a hundred years later it was believed that as an old man he wrote the Fourth Gospel in Ephesus. To say that a Galilean fisherman could never have written such a book begs the question about what kind of a book it is; the assertion is justifiable only if we agree (as in fact we do not) that it is the masterpiece of a philosophical genius, steeped in the reasonings of the Platonists and Stoics, who was attempting to divest the essential gospel of its Jewish wrappings in order to make it acceptable to the 'higher paganism' of the Hellenistic world. To say that it could not have been written by an eye-witness because he would have been too old assumes that we know when in fact it was written: if it had been written about AD 80, the eye-witness need not have been much more than seventy years old; and after all the main argument for a later date is the increasingly improbable one that the Gospel contains developed Gnostic views. Then, again, the work as we have it might have been written down by disciples who had often heard this venerable apostolic man expounding its themes at the weekly Eucharist—the men perhaps who have added their testimony in 21.24; in that case the Gospel might have been written at any date up to (say) AD 110. In short, we must be content to leave a considerable range of possibilities open.

THE GOSPEL IN THE NEW TESTAMENT CANON

The external evidence concerning the origins of the Fourth Gospel is, as we have said, tenuous and inconclusive. Only one affirmation about it can be made with confidence concerning the period before AD 150, namely, that it existed. It cannot incontrovertibly be proved to have been quoted by writers before that date, though there *may* be allusions to it in the Epistles of St Ignatius (martyred *c.* AD 107). A few passages in Justin Martyr (writing *c.* 155) may perhaps be said to make it probable that he had read the Gospel. Nevertheless extreme theories (e.g. those of A. Loisy followed by E. W. Barnes) that the Gospel was not written before the middle of the second century are rendered untenable by the discovery in Egypt in 1934 of a papyrus fragment of a manuscript of the Gospel, now in the Rylands Library in Manchester (Rylands Papyrus 457). This fragment contains only John 18.31-33, 37 f., five verses in all; and yet it is enough to dispose of all theories of a late origin of the Gospel. On palaeographical grounds the fragment must have been written some time between AD 125 and 150. This means that the Fourth Gospel was in circulation early in the second century, and indeed that it could have been written before the end of the first century. (See C. H. Roberts, *An Unpublished Fragment of the Fourth Gospel in the John Rylands Library*, 1935.) Another fragment (Egerton Papyrus 2), of an unknown apocryphal Gospel, is dated by the papyrologists *c.* 140-160; it also attests the existence of the Fourth Gospel in the first half of the second century. (See H. I. Bell and T. C. Skeat, *Fragments of an Unknown Gospel*, 1935). It is a remarkable fact that the manuscript evidence actually antedates any indubitable literary references; it is indeed remarkable that we have earlier manuscript evidence for St John's Gospel than for any other New Testament book!

This, however, only serves to deepen the mystery of its origin. If it was in circulation in the churches during the first half of the second century, and especially if it were known to be of apostolic origin, why was it so largely ignored? Of course, it would not have been regarded as authoritative unless it were understood to have been guaranteed by one at least of the apostles. Such a claim for the Fourth Gospel does not seem to have found general

acceptance until well into the latter half of the second
century. The Gospel was familiar to Melito, Bishop of
Sardis, who about AD 165 wrote a devotional homily on
'the Passion of the Lord', in which the allusions are un-
mistakable. Theophilus of Antioch (c. 180) is the first to
ascribe the Gospel to 'John"; he probably meant the
Apostle, but he does not say so. From this date onwards
the authorship of the Gospel by John the Apostle was
generally assumed, though it was still possible for heretical
groups like the Alogi in Asia Minor and for individuals
like Gaius the Presbyter in Rome to deny it even as late as
AD 200. St Irenaeus, Bishop of Lyons (died c. 200), the
first great Catholic theologian, opposed Gnostic heresy by
emphasizing the one true canon of Scripture as interpreted
by the unbroken apostolic tradition; and for him it was as
congruous with the providential ordering of things that
there should be four Gospels as that there should be four
winds of heaven or four corners of the earth. The Mura-
torian Canon—so called after its discoverer, L. A. Muratori
(1672-1750)—is a fragment of bad Latin which contains the
earliest known list of New Testament writings; its author
is unknown; J. B. Lightfoot and others have suggested
that it is a translation from the Greek of St Hippolytus
(c. 170-236). It gives a legendary account of how St Andrew
received a revelation that St John should write down all
that his fellow apostles remembered. The story is designed
to dispel any uneasiness about the discrepancies between
the Fourth Gospel and the other three: all the apostles had
a share in its composition, and in any case all the details
in all four Gospels are declared by the one Spirit. From the
end of the second century the Fourth Gospel was received
in East and West alike as the work of St John the Apostle,
the son of Zebedee.

EPHESUS AND JOHN THE ELDER

The tradition that the Apostle John lived in Ephesus to a great age is first encountered in Irenaeus's treatise *Against Heresies* (*c*. AD 180), where it is stated that he survived until the reign of Trajan. (Trajan succeeded Nerva in AD 98.) Irenaeus says explicitly that, after the other three Gospels had been written, 'John, the disciple of the Lord, who reclined on his bosom, issued his Gospel while residing at Ephesus.' He claims that he himself as a boy had listened to the teaching of St Polycarp, Bishop of Smyrna, who was martyred in AD 155 at the age of eighty-six; and he tells us that Polycarp as a youth had enjoyed intercourse with 'John and others who had seen the Lord'. This would appear to connect Irenaeus with the Apostle John at only one remove and thus to render his evidence highly trustworthy. But again there is a doubt. In the first place, there appears to have been another 'John' who figured prominently in the Church about the end of the first century. Papias, Bishop of Hierapolis in Asia Minor, who wrote probably about AD 140, is quoted by the historian Eusebius as having stated that, as a younger man, he had carefully tried to discover from those who had known 'the elders' what Andrew, Peter, Philip, Thomas, James, John or Matthew, 'or any other of the disciples of the Lord said, and the things which Aristion and John the Elder say'. The change of tense in this quotation is significant. John and the other apostles are spoken of in the past tense, but Aristion (about whom nothing more is known) and John the Elder were presumably still teaching in Papias's day. Now Irenaeus tells us that Papias was a hearer of John and a friend of Polycarp. Is it possible that Irenaeus was mistaken in thinking that John the Elder, whom Papias and Polycarp heard, was the Apostle? Is it significant that two of the three Epistles of John in the New Testament are explicitly said to be from 'the Elder' (II John 1; III John 1)?

In the second place, if John the Apostle had lived and taught in Ephesus until the reign of Trajan, it is strange that there is no reference to him in St Ignatius's Epistle to the Ephesians, written on his journey to his martyrdom in Rome (c. AD 107). He stresses the relationship of the Ephesians with the Apostle Paul, who had founded their church, but he seems to know nothing about their connection with the Apostle John. Yet by the time of Irenaeus it is generally assumed that the latter was a shining light of the Ephesian Church at the very time that Ignatius was Bishop of Antioch. Polycrates, Bishop of Ephesus from 189 to 198, seeking to establish the authority of the see of Ephesus, writes to Pope Victor claiming that amongst the 'great lights' who had fallen asleep (i.e. died) in Asia was 'John, who reclined upon the Lord's bosom' and who was buried in Ephesus. But since in the same passage Polycrates confuses Philip the Apostle with Philip the Evangelist, there is no assurance that he has not confused John the Apostle with John the Elder, especially since he had a strong motive for doing so. Polycrates's other statement that John 'as priest wore the sacred *petalon*', does not help us at all, since we do not know what it means. Probably it reflects the belief that John was a member of the Jewish high priestly caste and is an inference from John 18.16.

It is clear from this brief survey that no sure conclusions concerning the authorship of the Gospel can be drawn from the external evidence. Though the work was in existence in the first half of the second century, it does not seem to have been known to possess apostolic authority. It appears to have made its way, not on the name of its author or sponsor, but by the sheer power and attractiveness of its testimony to Christ—and this in an age when a considerable number of 'apocryphal' Gospels were in circulation and were competing for the recognition of the churches.

Once the Fourth Gospel had come to be widely appreciated, it was provided with apostolic credentials, the validity of which will probably always be a subject of debate amongst scholars. We may suppose that others besides Irenaeus found it useful in the struggle against the followers of the great second century Gnostic heretics, Basilides and Valentinus. But since its uncompromising testimony to the truth that the Word was made flesh and dwelt among us could be cited only if it could be held to possess apostolic authority, its association with the son of Zebedee would find increasing favour amongst orthodox believers. The Catholic Church rightly judged that its doctrine was truly apostolic as over against the Gnostic denial that the Word, which was God, had been made flesh in Jesus of Nazareth. Therefore, according to the standards prevailing in an age which did not and could not possess the methods of modern historical research, the Fourth Gospel was judged to be of apostolic origin, and circumstances combined to suggest that its apostolic guarantor must be John the son of Zebedee. What was being affirmed—and rightly—was that the Fourth Gospel bore true witness to the apostolic faith as against the novel doctrines of the heretics; and in the Church's decision to include the work in the canon of the New Testament Scriptures we may devoutly recognize a signal confirmation of its author's faith that the Spirit of truth would guide the Church of Christ into all truth. It is one of the ironies of modern New Testament scholarship that an influential school of criticism should have supposed that the Fourth Gospel is itself a work of Gnostic inspiration; but of this question Irenaeus is a better judge than Bultmann.

THE CHARACTER AND PURPOSE
OF THE GOSPEL

Since the external evidence is so inconclusive, the character and purpose of the Fourth Gospel must be ascertained primarily from its content. But in practice this means that each interpreter tends to find in the Gospel just what he is looking for, namely, the confirmation of his own ideas. Thus, Clement of Alexandria saw it as a ' spiritual Gospel ', entirely congenial to the mind of a Christianized Gnostic philosopher, while his contemporary Irenaeus found in it a valuable defence against Gnostic speculation. The differing attitudes of Clement and Irenaeus have their counterparts in the twentieth century. Many recent interpreters of the Gospel have claimed that the Fourth Evangelist, whose mind was imbued with Hellenistic philosophical notions, reinterpreted the Galilean gospel of Jesus and his earliest disciples in terms of the incipient Gnostic or even Mandaean cosmology of his day, and was thus a prime mover in the transformation of the original Jewish-Christian apocalyptic proclamation (or *kerugma*) of the primitive Christian community into the ' Gnostic Catholicism ' of Irenaeus and his orthodox contemporaries. R. Bultmann of Marburg, whose *Das Evangelium des Johannes* first appeared in 1923 (eleventh edition, 1950; an English translation is in preparation) is a leading exponent of these extreme views. In England C. H. Dodd, whose *Interpretation of the Fourth Gospel* (1953) contains a masterly survey of the Hellenistic religious *milieu*, more moderately regards the Gospel as an attempt to commend the Christian faith to the ' higher paganism ' of the Hellenistic world. On the other hand, others have stressed the Jewish character of St John's Gospel; and some have maintained, not perhaps convincingly, that an Aramaic substratum lies beneath the author's Greek.

Since the end of World War II a considerable amount of relevant but indirect new evidence has been coming to light; it will take a long time yet for it to be properly surveyed and assessed. It concerns both the Gnostic (Hellenistic) sects and the Jewish sects, more particularly the Essenes. If a conclusion may tentatively be drawn from this new material, it is that the New Testament documents —not least St John's Gospel—are much more original than many scholars had supposed. It now begins to appear that Gnosticism, even in its earliest days, was more pathetically and crudely fantastic even than Irenaeus and other ancient Christian writers had depicted it. Also the Jewish sects (like the Essenes) were more uncompromisingly and irrationally scrupulous and ascetic than anything we might have pictured about them from Pharisaic or Christian sources. Had we not come into possession of actual Gnostic and Essene literature—if, that is to say, we had remained dependent upon our Christian or Jewish sources of information—we might have gone on imagining that the Gnostics and the Essenes were really very like the Christians and the Jews, only a bit more pagan or a bit more fanatically Jewish as the case might be. We are now coming to see more clearly that such was not the case. The representation of St John as either a Christianized Gnostic or Jewish sectarian becomes less and less credible. The Fourth Evangelist stands out as *sui generis,* as a highly original thinker who owes little or nothing to Simon Magus and his like, on the one hand, or to the Essene 'Teacher of Righteousness' on the other. The more we find out about genuinely contemporary Hellenistic or Jewish religious movements, the further do St John and the other New Testament writers stand apart from them. When the Qumran discoveries were first announced ('the Dead Sea Scrolls'), it was widely given out that at last we should now be able to understand what had seemed to be genuinely original elements in the New Testament in the light of Essene theology and casuistry. It is the perennial illusion of scholars to suppose that they are now at last on the point of being able to classify some apparently creative thinker and to shew once for all that he was actually determined by this or that 'influence' or 'movement', until at length there is nothing original left in him at all. St John (like St Paul) has now for so long been 'explained' in terms of Hellenistic mysticism, or Persian dualism, or something of the kind, that the student of to-day is in danger of beginning with the assumption that his task is merely to analyse the Fourth Gospel into those Greek or Iranian or Jewish elements out of which an arch-syncretist had constructed his pantomime-horse of a Gospel.

The Qumran discoveries in 1947 and afterwards do not directly contribute to the solution of the 'problem' of St John's Gospel. But they are important in shewing that the Fourth Evangelist is much more Jewish than many had formerly supposed, and that certain of his ideas and expressions which had commonly been accounted Greek were in fact normal usage amongst the Essenes of the Dead Sea valley. Students of the Scrolls, who started from a conventional acceptance of Bultmann's hypotheses, which they had been taught from their youth, have come to realize that this Essene literature is a much more probable background against which the Fourth Gospel should be read than are Philo, the Hermetic *Corpus*, Gnosticism and so on. The 'dualism' of St John is not the metaphysical dualism of the Gnostics but the ethical dualism of the Essenes. No longer need we assume a late date for the Fourth Gospel on the ground that it shews the marked influence of developed (second century) Gnosticism. The evidence from Qumran makes it harder to think of St John as a philosophical Jew of the type of Philo; we no longer have need of such hypotheses, if the ways of thinking which we find in the Gospel are capable of being understood against a Palestinian background. This is not to say that the affinities of St John with the Qumran literature extend to anything more than the externals of language and forms of thought: there is nothing in all the known Gnostic or Qumran material which hints at such a figure as the Johannine Christ. In the whole range of ancient literature only the Synoptic Gospels can be said to contain any kind of approximation to the figure of the Word of God, who became incarnate in the historical Jesus of Nazareth, the son of Joseph (John 1.45). Those who wish to read more about the light thrown by recent discoveries upon the Fourth Gospel are recommended to read W. F. Albright's article, 'Recent Discoveries in Palestine and the Gospel of St. John' in *The Background of the New Testament and its Eschatology*, edited by W. D. Davies and D. Daube (Cambridge, 1956). They will also find a helpful contribution entitled 'The Qumran Scrolls and the Johannine Gospel and Epistles' in *The Scrolls and the New Testament*, edited by K. Stendahl (New York, 1957; London, 1958).

The point of view from which this Commentary is written is that we have in the Fourth Gospel a highly original presentation of the truth about Jesus Christ, made by a bold and profound thinker who has long reflected upon the tradition enshrined for us in the Synoptic Gospels. Like every other hypothesis—for instance, that the author was a syncretistic philosopher endeavouring to reconcile the Jewish-Christian *kerugma* with Hellenistic notions of a Gnostic Redeemer, or that he was a converted Greek literary man who had visited Palestine in search of local colour for his Gospel, apocryphal but *à la mode*—it must be judged by what kind of 'sense' it makes of all the available evidence. It is not possible for us to discuss here, or even to list, all the hypotheses which have been put forward; but it leads to clarity of judgment if we make our own point of view as explicit as possible. Our view is that the Fourth Gospel presents a profound and original meditation upon the tradition about Christ which was contained in the received (i.e. Synoptic) tradition concerning him. It is best regarded as itself a theological commentary upon the Synoptic tradition. The value of the book does not (in our view) reside in any new historical information which is not found in the Synoptic records. The acknowledgment that St John's is a highly original Gospel is not based upon and must not be confused with the assumption that he was in possession of an independent tradition of the life and teaching of the Lord—for example, a 'south Judaean' tradition as over against the 'Galilean' tradition of the Synoptists. Some critics have in the past sought to enhance the importance of the Fourth Evangelist as an independent witness by denying that he had read the Gospels of Matthew, Mark or Luke; but their arguments are unconvincing. As we shall see, it is more probable that St John knew the *content* of the Synoptic tradition, whether or not he had read the Synoptic Gospels in precisely the forms in which we now have them—a question which we must leave to the scholars. As we shall see, the value of his book lies in the way in which he decisively and compellingly brings out the true meaning of the received, the common, Gospel tradition, not an alternative to it. The Evangelist's 'inspiration' touches the interpretation of history rather than the recording of fresh historical facts. This does not mean that St John is any less an historian than are the Synoptic Evangelists, for all history-writing is concerned with the interpretation of facts. It is just here that what he has to teach us is so highly relevant to our problems to-day, since we live in an age which has not yet clarified its conception of revelation after the great revolution in theological method brought about by the coming-of-age of historical science in the nineteenth century. St John can teach us that the 'facts' of history are meaningless, if indeed they are knowable at all, apart from the exercise of the historical imagination through which revelation comes to us.

If it be true that St John's is an original mind, we must

be ready to be surprised and challenged by him. If he does
not challenge and surprise, there is no point in worrying
over the 'problem' of the Fourth Gospel. We should try
to be clear what this 'problem' really is. It is not just a
literary puzzle about authorship and date. It consists essentially in the shock of surprise which we get when we read
St John after having read the Synoptic Gospels. How are
we to account for such divergences and contrasts? At first,
perhaps, we may be disconcerted and even offended; we
may think that we have to choose between two histories,
St John *or* the Synoptists. Then we may suppose that, if
only we were clever enough, we could somehow harmonize
the two. Further reflection, it is to be hoped, will bring us
past these immature and inadequate stages, and we shall
begin to understand what it means to believe in a revelation
in *history*, a revelation, that is to say, not through philosophical speculation or mystical *gnosis*, but through the
testimony of those whose ears have heard, whose eyes have
seen, and whose hands have handled that which was from
the beginning concerning the Word of life (I John 1.1).
The 'problem' with which St John confronts us, and which
he will not let us escape, is the problem of a revelation
in history. If in the end we find that he thinks about the
Synoptic 'facts' in a way which is helpful to us amidst
our modern perplexities concerning revelation, the dis-
comfort of the surprise will be transformed into the joy
and serenity of a well-founded faith: 'blessed are they
that have not seen, and yet have believed' (John 20.29).
St John is for us to-day an exciting and stimulating teacher,
because we are finding out that he has addressed himself
to that very 'problem' of the relation of revelation and
history which fundamentalists on the one hand and modern-
ists on the other have despaired of solving. His boldness
in taking such surprising liberties with the received (or
Synoptic) tradition of the Church—which is indeed the
heart of the 'problem' of the Fourth Gospel—should

challenge us to understand, as he understands, that the truth of history is not at all the same thing as a literalistic record of historical 'facts'. St John, as we shall see, is concerned not so much with the bare recording of 'what happened' as with the saving meaning of the truth of history itself.

From our point of view then, it is important to try to see why St John has treated the Synoptic tradition as he has done. We must not allow ourselves to be distracted from this, the crucial, issue by conjectures and speculations which obscure the real problem—speculations about alternative sources of information, 'south Judaean traditions' and the like, which allow us to escape from the challenge of St John's radical treatment of the historical facts. By all means let the scholars search diligently and see if they can find genuine evidence for the existence of a non-Synoptic tradition that he may have used; but until such evidence is forthcoming let us not evade the real issue by assuming that such a tradition existed. Otherwise we shall be in danger of missing the lesson which St John has set out to teach us, namely, that historical 'facts', however well authenticated, are not themselves the life-giving Gospel; it is the interpreting Spirit, by whose activity the dead facts are made to live in believing hearts, which imparts the life of the Age to Come. New Testament criticism, if it be only an academic search for historical facts, is a labouring for the meat which perishes; and the task of Christian scholarship is quite other than this: 'This is the work of God, that ye believe on him whom he hath sent.' At every point the Fourth Evangelist is concerned with the interpretation of history, because *saving* truth is not historical knowledge as such—'the flesh profiteth nothing'—but is belief that the Father sent the Son to be the Saviour of the world.

It is this saving truth that the Fourth Evangelist has to teach us, whether or not he is the Apostle John or the Elder John known to Papias, and whether or not the Beloved

Disciple indeed wrote these things or is only a literary
device! In hiding from us his own name and face, the
Evangelist has confronted us with the surprise and challenge of the revelation in Jesus Christ, in whom we find,
not the answer to our literary and historical 'problems',
but the unfathomable mystery of life in his name. The finding of life is not a reward for our cleverness in solving
problems—problems which in fact are never likely to be
solved, since the decisive evidence has perished. The witness
of history does indeed confront us with many problems
which will occupy the attention of scholars for a long time
to come, but the apostolic witness involves a dimension that
is beyond scholarship as such, since it carries us out of the
region of problems into the realm of mystery. In the end
it is not with a problem that St John confronts us, but with
the mystery of our salvation. Scholars are equipped to
study problems, but it is childlike faith which perceives
mysteries: 'Ye must be born again.' That is doubtless
why St John writes not in the language of the philosophers
but in words which children can understand. We may perhaps fittingly conclude this introduction with some words
of Martin Luther which F. D. Maurice prefixed to his
Discourses on the Gospel of St John (1867):

'Johannes redet schlect und einfältig wie ein Kind, und
lauten seine Worte (wie die Weltweisen sie ansehen)
recht kindisch. Es ist aber eine solche Majestät drunter
verborgen, die kein Mensch, so hoch er auch erleuchtet
ist, erforschen noch ausreden kann' (*Auslegung des
Evangel. Johannis,* 1.5).[1]

---

[1] 'John speaks as simply and straightforwardly as a child, and his
words (as the wise men of the world regard them) sound very childish.
But within them there is hidden a majesty so great that no man, however profound his insight, can fathom or express it.'

NOTE ON GNOSTICISM AND MANDAEANISM

Gnosticism (from the Greek *gnosis,* knowledge) is properly a second-century Christian heresy associated with the names of Basilides, Valentinus and Marcion. It has, however, become customary, especially on the continent of Europe, to use the word of certain first century tendencies in the direction of Gnosticism. The danger about this way of speaking is that we too easily come to assume that a more-or-less developed form of Gnosticism had appeared before we have any definite evidence of it; and then finally we find ourselves speaking about Gnostic influences upon St Paul and St John, or constructing theories such as that the Fourth Gospel is an accommodation of primitive Christian beliefs to Hellenistic Gnostic speculations. The truth is that as yet we know very little about the embyronic 'Gnosticism' of the first century; but we are at least beginning to realize what a very complicated question the origin of Gnosticism is. More light on the subject is expected after the publication in due course of the Gnostic texts (mostly translations into Coptic from Greek) which were discovered in Upper Egypt in 1946 and which are now in the Coptic Museum at Cairo. Until recently we were dependent for our knowledge of Gnosticism upon theologians like Irenaeus, Tertullian and Hippolytus, who wrote against it.

Gnosticism seems to have been a mixture of ideas drawn from Greek philosophy on the one hand and from the oriental mystery-cults on the other; the mixture varies considerably from one practitioner to another. Two leading notions seem to be common to all its forms. First, the world of matter is evil, and salvation consists in deliverance from it into the world of light, which is the home of pure intelligences unsullied by contact with evil matter. Thus, such

Gnostics as Marcion declared that the world could not have been made by the High God, who being good could have no contact with defiling matter; it was made by an inferior and imperfect deity, or Demiurge, who was to be identified with the Jehovah of the Old Testament. Secondly, Gnosticism is essentially a doctrine of salvation by knowledge, whether this might mean at one end of the scale a philosophical knowledge of the eternal 'forms' of reality (cf. Platonism), or at the other end of it the possession of nonsensical abracadabra, magical pass-words which would enable the soul after death to elude the planetary guardians of the heavenly spheres and thus escape from the world of matter into the world of light. According to the so-called 'Gnostic myth' a heavenly Redeemer, or 'Light-Man', has descended from the world of light, living incognito here below and communicating to those able to understand the heavenly mysteries the saving knowledge which will be their passport into the blessed world above. Bultmann maintains that the Catholic doctrine of the incarnate Son of God, who came down from heaven, is only a Christianized version of the myth of the Gnostic Redeemer, and that the Fourth Evangelist and the unknown writer of the Epistles to the Ephesians and the Colossians were leading agents in the transformation of primitive Christianity into the second century Gnostic Catholicism of Irenaeus and later of the Nicene and Chalcedonian formularies. The chief difficulty in the way of his theory is that there is no evidence for the existence of the 'Gnostic myth' in the first century, save that supplied by the New Testament itself (chiefly the Fourth Gospel and Ephesians-Colossians). We shall see in the Commentary that the Fourth Gospel is susceptible of a very different interpretation and that it is more adequately understood in the light of its Old Testament and Hebraic background than in the shadows of Hellenistic syncretism.

The Mandaeans were a Gnostic sect whose obscure

origins are to be sought in the second or perhaps even the first century in the desert beyond the Jordan. John the Baptist figures prominently in their literature, and it is thought by some that they originated as a sect of his followers; others, however, think of them as a perverted Christian sect. They were ascetics who practised frequent baptisms (like the Essenes of Qumran), and this may have given rise to their veneration of the Baptist. Like other Gnostics they held that men's souls are imprisoned in their bodies but that they will achieve liberation through a Redeemer, who is called by different names. It would seem that they are in fact an Essene off-shoot which has been influenced by garbled versions of Christian doctrine. Their chief extant literature, the Ginza ('Treasure'), dates from the seventh or eighth century, and there are still to-day Mandaean communities in Iraq. (See further, C. H. Dodd, *The Interpretation of the Fourth Gospel*, pp. 115-30.) Now that the literature of the Essenes has come to light at Qumran, we hardly need to depend upon such late and hypothetical material for our knowledge of the 'background' of the Fourth Gospel. In our view the non-specialist reader of the Fourth Gospel may forget about the Gnostics and the Mandaeans.

BIBLIOGRAPHY

I. COMMENTARIES

*C. K. BARRETT, *The Gospel according to St John*, London, 1955.

*J. H. BERNARD, *The Gospel according to St. John*, International Critical Commentary, 2 vols., Edinburgh, 1928.

E. C. HOSKYNS, *The Fourth Gospel*, edited by F. N. Davey, 2nd edition in one vol., London, 1947.

R. H. LIGHTFOOT, *St John's Gospel: a Commentary*, Oxford, 1956.

R. H. STRACHAN, *The Fourth Gospel* (1917), 3rd edition revised and rewritten, London, 1941.

B. F. WESTCOTT, *The Gospel according to St John*, London, 1881; new reprint, London, 1958.

H. STRATHMANN, *Das Evangelium nach Johannes* (Das Neue Testament Deutsch), Göttingen, 1951.

* Commentaries on the Greek text.

II. FOR FURTHER READING

W. F. HOWARD, *The Fourth Gospel in Recent Criticism*, 4th edition revised by C. K. Barrett, London, 1955.

C. H. DODD and others, *Studies in the Fourth Gospel*, edited by F. L. Cross, London, 1957.

C. H. DODD, *The Interpretation of the Fourth Gospel*, Cambridge, 1953.

J. N. SANDERS, *The Fourth Gospel in the Early Church*, Cambridge, 1943.

P. GARDNER-SMITH, *St John and the Synoptic Gospels*, Cambridge, 1938.

H. ODEBERG, *The Fourth Gospel interpreted in its relation to Contemporaneous Religious Currents in Palestine and in the Hellenistic-Oriental World*, Uppsala and Stockholm, 1929.

W. TEMPLE, *Readings in St John's Gospel*, 1939 and 1940; both series in one vol., London, 1950.

The Commentary is based upon the Revised Version of 1884 (RV) and its margins (marg.), though sometimes reference is made to the Authorized Version of 1611 (AV). The latter is known as the King James Version in America. EVV indicates a reference to both these English Versions. LXX stands for the Septuagint Greek translation. OT stands for Old Testament; NT for New Testament.

COMMENTARY

I

THE PROLOGUE

1.1-18

The first eighteen verses of St. John's Gospel are commonly called 'the Prologue'. They constitute a theological meditation upon the meaning of the fact of Christ. Who is he? The answer is that he is none other than the eternal Wisdom of God, by whom the world was made. His coming and character are foretold by the scriptural writers of old, and he is called by them THE WORD OF GOD or THE WISDOM OF GOD. The amazing truth is that the eternal Word (or 'Wisdom') has in Jesus Christ taken flesh, and has thus revealed the transcendent God in the only way in which men could have 'seen' him, namely, in human form.

1. In the beginning

The words deliberately recall Gen. 1.1, IN THE BEGINNING GOD CREATED THE HEAVEN AND THE EARTH. One of the great Johannine themes is that Christ is the incarnation of the Word or Wisdom of God by whom the world was made (Ps. 33.6; Prov. 8.22-31) and by whom the new creation of the end-time shall be consummated (Rev. 3.14). Christ is both the beginning and the end, the Alpha and the Omega (Rev. 1.8; 21.6; 22.13). He is the goal (THE AMEN, Rev. 3.14) as well as the origin of the world-process. All things come from him and go to him. The Christ-event, which is the theme of the Gospel, is the beginning of the new creation; though it is staged in ordinary, secular history, it is the first act of the drama which will be played out on a cosmic stage, when the history of this world is concluded, by him who has declared through his Spirit in the Church, BEHOLD, I MAKE ALL THINGS NEW (Rev. 21.5). The Church on earth is the beginning of the new creation of the end-time, into which has been breathed the breath of life (John 20.22; cf. Gen. 2.7).

the Word

The Greek word (*logos*) means 'rational utterance', either a single word or a message. It is a communication from one rational being to another. The basic idea springs from the Genesis creation-story: AND GOD SAID, LET THERE BE . . . (Gen. 1.3, 6, 9, 11, etc.). God created the world by simply speaking the *word* of command; he did not have to make it with his hands out of some pre-existent matter, like Plato's Demiurge. The biblical doctrine of creation *ex nihilo* by divine *fiat* is a supreme poetical representation of the absolute transcendence and power of the Creator-God: he needs only to utter his will, and it is accomplished. Cf. Ps. 33.6, 9: BY THE WORD OF THE LORD WERE THE HEAVENS MADE, AND ALL THE HOST OF THEM [i.e. the stars] BY THE BREATH OF HIS MOUTH. . . . FOR HE SPAKE AND IT WAS DONE; HE COMMANDED AND IT STOOD FAST (cf. also Ps. 147.18 f.; Isa. 55.11). Neither Gen. 1 nor John 1 is offering us a philosophical explanation of the creation of the universe; they are giving supreme poetical expression to the biblical awareness of the utter dependence of all things upon God. St. John perceives the dependence of the whole world upon the creative Word of God, whose glory had now been revealed in Christ.

the Word was with God, and the Word was God

In some passages in the Wisdom books (see esp. Job 28. 20-28; Prov. 8. 22-31; Wisd. 7.22–8.1; Ecclus. 24.1-12) the creative Word of God is personified under the figure of Wisdom (Gk., *sophia*). The conception is poetic rather than metaphysical; that is to say, it is a way of speaking about the activity of the utterly transcendent God, as later Judaism had come to understand him, and of how such a transcendent Being could be active in the creation and providential ordering of the world. Wisdom is not to be thought of as a second god, an intermediary between the far-off transcendent God and the material world. It is rather a means of avoiding anthropomorphism: God must not be pictured in human form, making the world with his hands as a potter makes a vessel. It is nevertheless an affirmation that God did make the world and still orders and controls it, but it is a poetic way of affirming this mystery, which men could not have grasped with their rational intellect. St John never uses the word 'wisdom' (*sophia*), probably because he wished to dissociate himself from Hellenistic speculation, which made great play with the notion of emanations or intermediaries, such as *gnosis* (knowledge) and *sophia*, which bridged the chasm between this world-order and the far-off, unknowable, transcendent, divine Being of Greek philosophy. St Paul, on the other hand, has no hesitation in describing Christ as the Wisdom of God (I Cor. 1.24, 30; Col. 2.3), whereas he never calls him the Word of God; yet both Paul and John are affirming the same truth. St John's phrase, THE WORD WAS WITH GOD, and his affirmation that all things were made by the Word (v. 3) are reminiscent of such passages as Prov. 8.30, I WAS BY HIM AS A MASTER WORKMAN (in its context). Christ is the creative power of God made visible in terms of human life. But St John goes further than any of the OT Wisdom writers when he declares that THE WORD WAS GOD. He wishes to rule out the Hellenistic notion of *sophia* or the Stoic notion of the immanent *logos* as a kind of second god, intermediate between the High God and the material world. Christ is not other than God.

4. In him was life . . . light

Rabbinic Judaism had identified Wisdom with Torah

(the Law); Wisdom had made her home (or TABERNACLE) in Israel (read Ecclus. 24. 1-12 and esp. v. 23). Torah, said the rabbis, is light and life (cf. Ps. 119.105; Prov. 6.23; John 5.39). One of the main concerns of the Fourth Gospel is to show that not Torah but Christ is light and life. The archetypal light of the Creation (Gen. 1.3), of which the sun itself is but the counterpart in the firmament (Gen. 1.14-19), shall shine again in all its pristine brightness in the end-time: in the heavenly Jerusalem there is no need of sun or moon because the divine glory lightens it AND THE LAMP THEREOF IS THE LAMB (Rev. 21.23; 22.5; cf. Isa. 60.19 f.). The light which was in the beginning shall be again at the end, and that light is Christ. Life also, which God breathed into mankind at the Creation (Gen. 2.7), shall be supremely the characteristic of the end-time ('the life of the Age to Come').

5. light shineth in the darkness

Between the creation-light in the beginning and the glory-light of the end-time there intervenes a period of darkness: the world has been invaded and conquered by the powers of evil or of DARKNESS. Christ, THE TRUE LIGHT, the light of the end-time, IS ALREADY SHINING (I John 2.8; cf. John 8.12; 9.5; 12.35 f., 46), and the dark powers of evil can neither understand nor overcome him (APPREHEND in the original has both meanings).

6. a man sent from God

In view of the existence of a widespread sect of John the Baptist's followers (cf. Acts 19.1-7, the twelve disciples of John *at Ephesus*) it was necessary to assert that the Baptist was not himself the TRUE LIGHT but was the WIT-NESS OF THE LIGHT. The significance of the Baptist was that he pointed away from himself and towards Christ (vv. 7 f., 15, 26, 29-36; 3.26-30; 10.41). The whole NT agrees that the Baptist was sent 'from God'; he was a divinely

appointed sign that the consummation of the divine purpose, as foretold by the prophets, was at hand (e.g. Matt.
11.7-13; 17.10-13; Mark 11.29-33; Luke 1.5-25).

9. every man coming into the world

The phrase is an idiom meaning 'every mortal man'.
The light shines upon all men, whether they recognize it
or not, and their deeds are judged by it: it is one of the
functions of light in the Fourth Gospel to 'shew up' evil
and thus to effect judgment (John 3.19-21; cf. I Cor. 4.5;
Eph. 5.13). It is highly improbable that St John is here
enunciating the Stoic view that all men are illuminated by
the divine *Logos* (Reason); such a doctrine is strongly
contradicted in v. 10. The meaning is that the TRUE LIGHT
judges all men.

10. the world

Because THE WORLD (*kosmos*) had fallen under the
powers of darkness, it did not recognize the creative Word
which brought it into existence when he came into it (at
the incarnation of the Word in Christ). THE WORLD or THIS
WORLD is a very common expression in St John; it usually
means this present world (as contrasted with the world to
come), which is alienated from God and LIETH IN THE EVIL
ONE (I John 5.19), and which yet paradoxically remains
the world which God loves and which he sent his Son to
save (John 3.16 f.; 4.42; 12.47; I John 4.14).

11. his own

The Greek text says that he came to (claim) his own
property (see RV marg.) but that his own people rejected
him; cf. Mark 6. 1-6; 12.1-12. The next verse, however,
indicates that there were *some* who received him.

12. the right to become children of God

The reference here is to Christian baptism. The next

verse draws a contrast between our first birth (*of bloods*, i.e. of this or that particular human stock; of carnal desire; of the will of the male) and our second birth at baptism (of the will of God). The contrast between our natural birth and our birth FROM ABOVE (or AGAIN) is reasserted in John 3.3-7, where the baptismal reference is very clear. It is in our baptism that we become children of God.

13. born . . . of God

There may well be an allusion here to the Virgin Birth of Christ, though the verse can hardly be cited as historical evidence for it. It does, however, fit exceedingly well into the pattern of such a doctrine: Christians in their baptism are born, as Christ himself was born, not of human paternity but OF GOD. (Some early Latin texts make the whole verse refer to Christ and not to Christians: *qui . . . natus est*, in the singular; but this is doubtless the consequence of the parallel between Christian baptism and the Virgin Birth of Christ having been noticed by some copyist or translator.)

14. And the Word became flesh

In these simple words the whole profound mystery and miracle of the Christian faith is expressed. The meaning is not that the Wisdom-Word was changed into flesh but that he took a robe or body of flesh, or, in a word, God (for the Word *was* God) became man. The word FLESH in this context means 'human nature'. The opening words of *The Riddle of the NT* by Edwyn Hoskyns and F. N. Davey (1931) may be allowed to stand as the appropriate comment on this incomparable text: 'When the Catholic Christian kneels at the words *incarnatus est* or at the words *and was incarnate*, he marks with proper solemnity his recognition that the Christian religion has its origin not in general religious experience, nor in some peculiar esoteric mysticism, nor in a dogma. He declares his faith to rest upon a particular event in history. . . . This is Christian orthodoxy, both Catholic and Protestant.' Or one might quote the seventeenth century poet:

> ' Behold the great Creator makes
> Himself a house of clay,
> A robe of Virgin flesh he takes
> Which he will wear for ay.'

and dwelt amongst us

The Greek word is TABERNACLED (RV marg.), lit. ' lived in a tent '. In the days of the redemption of Israel from Egypt the divine glory had tabernacled in visible brightness (Ex. 40.34-38); and the Scriptures promised that in the latter days the visible GLORY of God would reappear and be seen by all nations (e.g. Isa. 35.2; 40.5; 66.18). God would again tabernacle with men; cf. Ezek. 37.27, MY TABERNACLE ALSO SHALL BE WITH THEM, AND I WILL BE THEIR GOD. In his vision of the new heavens and new earth at the end-time St John sees this prophecy fulfilled: BEHOLD, THE TABERNACLE OF GOD IS WITH MEN, AND HE SHALL TABERNACLE WITH THEM . . . AND BE THEIR GOD (Rev. 21.3; cf. 7.15). The incarnation ('enfleshment', from the Latin *caro, carnis*, flesh) of the Word in Christ was for St John the first act in the final redemption-drama of the end-time: God's promise was fulfilled, for he had tabernacled with men in the flesh of Jesus Christ and now continues to tabernacle on earth in Christ's resurrection-body, the Church (John 2.19-22). The Jews boasted that Wisdom tabernacled in the Torah in Israel (Ecclus. 2.8, 10, 23); St John makes a higher claim, namely, that God himself tabernacles with men in Christ and his Church.

we beheld his glory

The word ' we ' is not intended as an assertion of eyewitness authority; it means ' we who possess the faith of the apostles ' (cf. I John 1.1-3). The glory of Christ in this age is veiled except to the eye of faith; at his coming (parousia; cf. I John 2.28) in his unveiled glory at the end-time EVERY EYE SHALL SEE HIM, including those who rejected and crucified him (Rev. 1.7). It was only to his disciples that the incarnate Word manifested his glory (John 2.11); THE WORLD did not receive the revelation at all (John 14.22). The fundamental biblical meaning of GLORY (*doxa*) is 'the visible brightness of the divine presence'; the concept is closely associated, as we have noted, with the pentateuchal stories of the visible brightness of God's presence in the Tabernacle in the Wilderness, when he dwelt with men (Ex. 25.8 f.; 29.43-46; 40.35). The *visible* brightness of God's presence was now in this age withdrawn, but the Scriptures promised that it would be restored in the latter days: THE LATTER GLORY OF THIS HOUSE SHALL BE GREATER THAN THE FORMER (Hag. 2.7-9). St John claims that for the eye of faith this promise is already fulfilled.

only begotten

The expression means that Christ is Son of the Father in a unique sense (cf. the Synoptic BELOVED SON, Mark 1.11; 9.7; 12.6, and parallels). Christians are SONS OF GOD (cf. John 1.12) in a derivative sense; or, as St Paul would say, they are *adopted* sons (Rom. 8.15; Gal. 4.5). Christians have the 'right' to become sons of God only because Christ is *the* Son of God by right.

full of grace and truth

GRACE occurs in the Fourth Gospel only in the Prologue; TRUTH is a frequent Johannine word. The phrase means that God's faithfulness to his covenant-promise (which is the usual meaning of 'grace' in the OT) has resulted in the final truth-revelation now given by the incarnate Word. 'Truth' for St John means the liberating, saving revelation of God in Christ (cf. 8.32).

15. he was before me

The Baptist attests the pre-existence of the eternal Word (cf. John 8.56-8).

16. grace for grace

' The meaning of this phrase seems to be that Christian life is based at all points upon grace; as it proceeds, one grace is exchanged only for another' (C. K. Barrett, p. 140).

17. the law was given by Moses

Torah is not, as the rabbis claimed, light, life, living water, bread from heaven, the way or the truth; it is Christ who is all these things, as the rest of the Gospel will go on to shew. The contrast between law and grace is almost Pauline here. Law, which cannot save, was given by (or through) Moses; the covenanted, saving truth of God came by (or through) Jesus Messiah.

18. No man hath seen God

The invisible God has been revealed in Christ. The Fourth Gospel makes considerable play upon the idea of ' seeing ' with the natural eye (or reason) and ' seeing ' with the eye of faith; e.g. John 9.37-41; 14.9; 20.29. St John denies that ' seeing is believing'; he would say rather that believing is seeing.

the bosom of the Father

A striking metaphor, emphasizing the unity and communion of the Father and the Son; cf. John 10.30; 14.10; 16.28; 17.21, 26.

THE WITNESS OF JOHN

1.19-34

Long before the Fourth Gospel was written a sect of the Baptist's followers had been widely established and its emissaries had reached Ephesus (cf. Acts 19.1-7). It was therefore necessary for the Christian mission to stress John's own account of himself as the forerunner whose function was to witness to Christ.

21. Art thou Elijah?
The rabbis taught that before the Messiah came, and before the expected outpouring of the Spirit took place in the Messianic age, Elijah, who had not died but had been taken up into heaven (II Kings 2.11), would return to warn God's people that the Messianic judgment, the DAY OF THE LORD, was at hand, in accordance with the promise of Mal. 3.1-3 and 4.5 f. (cf. Mark 9.11, THEY ASKED HIM, SAYING, THE SCRIBES SAY THAT ELIJAH MUST COME FIRST). The Synoptic Gospels represent John as giving point to his proclamation that the Kingdom of God was at hand and that the judgment was about to begin by dressing the part of Elijah (the camel's hair, leather girdle, etc.; Mark 1.6; cf. II Kings 1.8). St Matthew and St Mark make Jesus himself assert that the Baptist was the expected Elijah (Matt. 17. 11-13; Mark 9.12 f.). St Luke in his birth narratives says of the infant John that he will go IN THE SPIRIT AND POWER OF ELIJAH (Luke 1.17; cf. Mal. 4.6; Ecclus. 48.10), but later in his Gospel drops the John-Elijah parallel, doubtless because he wishes to represent Christ himself as the new Elijah. St John here makes the Baptist categorically deny that he is Elijah, possibly from the same motive, though he nowhere develops the parallelism of Elijah-Christ. Perhaps he considers the Herod-Ahab,

Herodias-Jezebel theme of popular Christian belief (cf. Mark 6.14-29) rather crude and superstitious.

Art thou the prophet?

That is, the prophet like Moses, the 'new Moses', whose coming Moses himself had prophesied; cf. Deut. 18.15, 18, THE LORD THY GOD WILL RAISE UP UNTO THEE A PROPHET . . . LIKE UNTO ME; TO HIM SHALL YE HEARKEN (cf. also John 1.25, 45; 4.14). John denies that he is the new Moses; the NT affirms that Christ is THE PROPHET in this sense (e.g. Acts 3.22).

23. The voice of one crying in the wilderness

The Baptist's own account of himself implies that he is indeed SENT FROM GOD as the fulfilment of scriptural prophecy concerning the latter days: he is the Isaianic prophet who proclaims the drawing nigh of the salvation of God (Isa. 40.3; cf. also Matt. 3.3 and parallels). He does not claim to be either the new Moses or the new Elijah.

26. I baptize with water

St John, of course, is thinking of the contrast between the Baptist's water-baptism and the Messianic baptism in Holy Spirit (cf. Mark 1.8; Acts 1.5; 11.16). The casual reader of the Fourth Gospel hardly notices that it does not mention the actual baptism of Jesus by John. It has been conjectured that the evangelist's silence on the point is due to his fear that it might suggest that in some way John was superior to Jesus (cf. Matt. 3.14 f.); but this is not likely. It is more probable that he does not mention the baptism for the same reason that he does not explicitly mention the institution of the Eucharist, namely, his view that the two are sacraments or mysteries which must not be spoken of in a book which pagans are likely to read. The earliest Christians jealously guarded the sacraments from profane eyes. As we shall see, the Fourth Gospel nevertheless contains a good deal of instruction about both sacraments without explicitly mentioning them.

28. Bethany beyond Jordan

There seem to have been two places called Bethany, and the matter has caused confusion since at least the third century AD; compare John 10.40 with 11.1 and 11.18. Bethabarah, etc. (RV marg.), seem like early attempts to remove the confusion by finding another name for the Transjordanian Bethany. It is more important that we should notice that the Baptist baptized *beyond* Jordan in order to symbolize the truth that the Jews by their disobedience had forfeited their claim to be sons of Abraham (cf. Matt. 3.9) and had therefore to re-enter the Promised Land by going through Jordan anew.

29. Behold, the lamb of God

This figure fuses together in a single profound symbol several different OT conceptions and Jewish religious practices. (*a*) God has fulfilled the promise foreshadowed in the offering of Isaac (Gen. 22.8; God has provided the lamb for sacrifice). (*b*) Christ is the Christian passover lamb (Ex. 12; cf. I Cor. 5.7, OUR PASSOVER-LAMB HAS BEEN SACRIFICED, NAMELY CHRIST). (*c*) Christ is the Suffering Servant of Isaianic prediction (Isa. 53.7, A LAMB THAT IS LED TO THE SLAUGHTER; cf. Acts 8.32). (*d*) Christ is the Conqueror: in later Jewish apocalyptic imagery the bellwether leads and defends the flock, routing its enemies (cf. the victorious Lamb of Rev. 14.1, 4). (*e*) A lamb was offered in the Temple at the daily sacrifice (the burnt offering). The Lamb in the Johannine symbol combines all these allusions, but the image of the passover lamb is dominant, despite the fact that the Jewish passover sacrifice was not expiatory. Here it is stressed that Christ is the Christian expiatory sacrifice for sin (WHICH TAKETH AWAY THE SIN OF THE WORLD). The Book of Revelation provides the explanation. There the figure of the Lamb slain is a eucharistic symbol: the Lamb slain is worshipped at the heavenly Liturgy (Rev. 5.6, 8 f., 12 f.), as still the Church on earth at the Eucharist chants the *Agnus Dei*. The Eucharist is the Christian passover-feast; Christ, the Christian passover lamb, does that which the Jewish passover and all the rest of the Jewish sacrifices could never do: by his self-oblation he bore the sin of the world: THOU WAST SLAIN AND DIDST PURCHASE UNTO GOD WITH THY BLOOD MEN OF EVERY TRIBE, AND TONGUE AND PEOPLE AND NATION. . . . (Rev. 5.9). The underlying theological unity of the Fourth Gospel and the Revelation of St John is here clearly illustrated, despite the linguistic dissimilarities; they use different Greek words for ' lamb ', thus presenting the literary critics with a further puzzle.

32. the Spirit descending as a dove

St John, as we have noted, does not record the baptism of Jesus, but these words indicate that he is well aware that it took place, since the descent of the Spirit as a dove happened when Jesus came up out of the water (Mark 1.10). St Mark (1.10) and St Matthew (3.16) say only that Jesus saw the vision of the dove; St Luke (3.22), however, says that the dove descended IN BODILY FORM, and St John tells us that the Baptist saw the vision.

33. he that baptizeth with the Holy Spirit

Later Judaism taught that in the Messianic Age God would pour out his Holy Spirit upon a renewed Israel (Joel 2.28 f.; Isa. 32.15; Ezek. 39.29; Zech. 12.10). The apostolic Church claimed that this prophecy had been fulfilled (Acts 2.16-18; 10.45; Rom. 5.5; Gal. 4.6; Eph. 4.7 f.; Titus 3.6). This outpouring of the Spirit could not and did not happen until after the death and resurrection of Christ (cf. John 7.39; 20.22). The Spirit is given to every individual Christian in his baptism, and it is Christ himself who

imparts the gift; Christ, as the Baptist himself confesses, is
HE THAT BAPTIZETH WITH THE HOLY SPIRIT (cf. Acts 19.2, 6).

34. the Son of God

In Mark 1.11 it is the Voice from Heaven which testifies
that Jesus is the Son of God; the Baptist is here represented
as making this divine testimony his own. In Greek usage
the term 'son of God' might mean nothing more than
'righteous man'; and, of course, the Emperor was *Divi
Filius*. But in Christian usage the expression 'Son of God'
carries the highest Christological significance; it implies
that Christ is of the same substance as God, or is essentially
and uniquely divine. It is used in this sense by St John
throughout his Gospel. The NT usage is based chiefly on
that of the OT, where Israel is God's 'son' (Ex. 4.22 f.;
Hos. 11.1). But the essence of sonship is obedience to the
father's will (Mal. 1.6), and Israel had been disobedient (cf.
John 8.41-44); Jesus, however, is perfectly conformed to the
will of the Father (John 4.34; 5.30; 6.38; 14.31), and hence
is truly and uniquely the Son of God.

THE DISCIPLES OF JOHN AND
THE DISCIPLES OF JESUS

1.35-51

There is no possibility of harmonizing St John's account
with those of the Synoptists. It is not merely that John 1.40
is hard to reconcile with Mark 1.16; it might be argued (if
anyone thought it worth while to do so) that St John is
expanding in fuller detail what St Mark has condensed
into a sentence. The real difficulty is this: in St. Mark's
account a long time elapses before the disciples, who are
upbraided for their 'blindness', recognize that Jesus is

the Christ, and even then they are commanded to be silent
(Mark 8.29 f.); but in St John it is proclaimed from the
very beginning that Jesus is the Son of God, the Lamb of
God, the Messiah, the King of Israel and the Son of Man—
all these titles occur in the first chapter. In St John, the
Baptist has experienced a divine revelation concerning the
mystery of the person of Jesus (1.33), whereas in the
Synoptists he sends messengers from prison to ask whether
Jesus is HE THAT SHOULD COME (i.e. the Messiah). In St
John Jesus publicly debates with 'the Jews' the mystery
of his person and mission in a manner that has no parallel
in his discussions with the Pharisees in the Synoptists. Once
we recognize and reflect upon these things, it becomes clear
to us that St John is not writing an alternative account of
the life of Christ, which aims at correcting or replacing the
Gospel of St Mark (or its revised and enlarged editions, St
Matthew and St Luke). He is writing a theological meditation upon the Synoptic Gospel-tradition, not a rival version of it. He is concerned not to tell the historical story
since the Synoptic tradition, well known throughout the
churches, had done that already; his aim is to bring out the
truth of history, to shew the signficance of those matters
which were firmly embedded in the tradition of the life
and words of the Lord Jesus, as taught in every place where
the *kerugma* (proclamation) had been preached. St John's
Gospel is a re-telling of the Gospel story from the point
of view of the Church which has experienced the power
of the risen, ascended and glorified Christ, and which
rejoices in the 'comfort' of the Spirit of truth. The glory-
light shines upon Christ from the beginning of the story.
There is no account of the Transfiguration in St John's
Gospel; St John explains the significance of Christ's person
by shining upon it the transfiguring light of the glory of
God, as the eyes of the believing Church now see it, at
every stage of the Gospel story. Thus, the Baptist hails
him as LAMB OF GOD and SON OF GOD, for these are the

two truths which emerge most clearly from the encounter
of Jesus and John; Andrew declares, WE HAVE FOUND THE
MESSIAH; and Nathaniel acknowledges that Rabbi Jesus
is SON OF GOD and KING OF ISRAEL, because this is the
meaning which underlay the first vital meeting of the Lord
with his disciples. The Fourth Evangelist, in short, is bringing out, in his own deeply poetic and allusive way, the
truth of the history that the Synoptic tradition enshrines;
he never for a moment intended to substitute for it a
'Johannine' tradition, which could be compared and contrasted and checked and balanced in the scales of historians,
as if it were of the same *genre* as the Synoptic record.

35. on the morrow

There is probably some deep meaning in the careful
time-scheme of this section (the phrase occurs in vv. 29 and
43 also; cf. v. 39, IT WAS ABOUT THE TENTH HOUR); but, if
so, no one has succeeded in explaining what it is.

36. they followed Jesus

If St John is preserving an historical tradition here, two
at least (including St Andrew) of the disciples of Jesus
had been followers of the Baptist. This is by no means
improbable, since after all the Synoptic tradition is highly
condensed and gives us no information at all about the
previous lives of the disciples. On the other hand, St John
may merely be representing in one of his historical figures
the truth that the correct understanding of the Baptist's
proclamation compels the recognition that Jesus is the
Christ and that all who have HEARD John's real message
will follow Jesus.

38. Rabbi

The common title of the Jewish teachers of the Law. It
is one of the unexplained mysteries of the whole Gospel
tradition why Jesus, an untrained (so far as we are told)

village carpenter, should be accorded this title and invited to perform the functions of a rabbi (Mark 1.22; Luke 4.31 ff.). St John usually translates Hebrew and Aramaic words into Greek; see vv. 41 f., and also 4.25; 9.7; 11.16; 19.17; 20.16, 24; 21.2. The expression in EVV BEING INTERPRETED simply means in modern English ' being translated '.

where abidest thou?

The verb ' to abide ' bears such pregnant meaning in the Fourth Gospel that here and in the next verse we must understand a deep spiritual significance to be intended. ' To abide with ' Jesus means not only to share his teaching and his fellowship but actually in some sense to become one with him (cf. John 15.4-10).

41. his own brother Simon

It may be that the ' call ' of Peter and Andrew was not so sudden as it appears in Mark 1.16-18, which gives no explanation at all of how it came about that they left their nets so abruptly. St Mark is very condensed, and he is not interested in biographical details. St John may preserve a genuine tradition that it was Andrew who first introduced his brother to Jesus. In any case, St John wants it to be understood that the correct response to the recognition of Christ's Messiahship is a life of missionary service in the task of propagating the good news. St Andrew has become in Christian symbolism the ' patron saint ' of all the missionaries of Christ.

We have found the Messiah

This is the message of the Christian missionaries in every age. Though the conception of the Messiah is Hebrew and requires for its understanding a sound knowledge of the Hebrew Scriptures, it must nevertheless be proclaimed and explained to all nations. The OT, with its teaching concerning the Christ who should come, in whom the purpose of the ages was to be accomplished, is no longer a Jewish book; it belongs to Christians, because it testifies of Christ (John 5.39). The coming of the expected Christ, and the outpouring of the Spirit in the Messianic Age which he would inaugurate, were accepted doctrines in every type of contemporary Judaism, except the Sadducean; John the Baptist had proclaimed the imminence of this consummation of the prophetic expectation. Now the Christian missionaries proclaim 'We have found the Christ'—and they bring men and women to Jesus.

42. the son of John
Or 'Joanes' or 'Jonas'; see Matt. 16.17; John 21.15-17.

Cephas
An Aramaic word meaning 'rock' or 'stone', corresponding to the Greek word *petra*. If the translators of EVV had really translated the Greek into English, we should have read 'thou shalt be called Cephas, which is by interpretation Rock-man'. St John gives no reason for the renaming of Simon, such as that he is the *foundation-stone* of the Church (Matt. 16.18) or that he is to be of rock-like integrity.

43. Philip
That a native of Bethsaida should bear a Greek name like Philip shews how far Greek culture and language had penetrated Galilean life. Philip appears in St Mark's list of the Twelve (Mark 3.18 and parallels), but the Synoptists record no incidents in which he is named; cf. John 6.7; 12.21 f.; 14.8 f. He should not be confused with Philip the Evangelist (Acts 6.5; 8.5-40; 21.8).

45. Philip findeth Nathanael
When Philip receives his call, his immediate response (like Andrew's) is to proclaim the truth to someone else.

The name Nathanael is purely Hebraic and means 'God has given'; there may be deep meaning here, for in the thought of St John the disciples are those whom God has given to Christ (e.g. 17.6, 9 etc.). Nathanael does not appear in the Synoptists' lists of the Twelve, and it has often been supposed that he is the same person as Bartholomew. Indeed, the only other reference to him in the NT occurs in the 'appendix' to the Fourth Gospel (21.2), where we learn that he was a native of Cana in Galilee.

of whom Moses in the law, and the prophets, did write

The reference to the Law (i.e. the Pentateuch) is, of course, to Deut. 18.15, 18; see the note above on v. 21 (THE PROPHET). The apostolic Church is convinced that all the prophets of Israel foretold the coming of Jesus Christ (e.g. Luke 24.44; Acts 3.24; I Peter 1.10 f.).

the son of Joseph

In John 6.42 the Jews bring forward the fact that Jesus is the son of Joseph in disproof of his divine claim. The fact that St John records that Jesus was popularly believed to be Joseph's son does not imply that St John believed it, and that therefore he did not know of the doctrine of the Virgin Birth of Christ.

46. can any good thing come out of Nazareth?

The form of this question indicates contempt of Nazareth because Nazareth is in Galilee; the rabbis of Jerusalem had put it about that no light could be expected from that despised quarter (7.41, 52), and their view was echoed even by a native of Cana.

47. An Israelite indeed, in whom is no guile

Jesus is represented as having supernatural knowledge of others (so in v. 50 below; cf. also 2.25). The word ISRAELITE is used by St John only here, and it is to be contrasted with his frequent deprecatory use of THE JEWS. In all probability Nathanael is being set up as the new type of the true Israel, as contrasted with the old Israel (i.e. Jacob, who stole his brother's birthright, Gen 27), in whom there was much guile.

48. Nathanael is convinced by the intimate knowledge of him which Jesus possesses, though the precise circumstances of the encounter are not very clearly explained; he makes his confession of faith in Christ in the following verses. St John is sure that Jesus possessed supernatural insight into the character and conduct of other people (cf. 1.42; 2.25; 4.17-19, 39; 13.10 f., 21, 26).

49. Son of God . . . King of Israel

Both of these are titles of the Messiah; the Messiah was frequently referred to as God's Son (cf. John 11.27; II Sam. 7.14; Pss. 2.7; 89.26 f.) and also as Israel's King (cf. John 12.13; Zeph. 3.15; Zech. 9.9). In St John's view Jesus is indeed KING OF ISRAEL but rejects the title KING OF THE JEWS (John 6.15; 18.33-37). His Kingdom is not limited to one section of the world; he is the Universal King, a truth emphasized in the Apocalypse (Rev. 16.14; 19.16).

50. underneath the fig tree

It has often been suggested that the fig tree here must be figurative, since in the OT it is a frequent poetic symbol of Israel. The verse would thus mean that Jesus had known Nathanael for a period of time before he was converted to faith in Christ. Such conjectures are not entirely convincing.

51. the angels of God ascending and descending

This obscure saying probably means that Nathanael, the type of the true 'Israelite' of the new order, would have his faith confirmed in a vision comparable to the vision seen by the first 'Israelite', namely Jacob, who at Bethel saw THE ANGELS OF GOD ASCENDING AND DESCENDING upon the ladder to heaven (Gen. 28.12). This opening of the heavens of which Jesus speaks probably refers to the cataclysmic events of the Parousia (cf. Mark 14.62), a consummation which is always present to the mind of the Johannine writer(s).

Son of Man

The use of this strange self-designation of Jesus at this point confirms the view that the opening of the heavens here means the Parousia, when men would SEE THE SON OF MAN COMING IN CLOUDS WITH GREAT POWER AND GLORY (Mark 13.26; cf. Dan. 7.13; Mark 14.62; Rev. 1.7; 14.14). Whatever else Jesus may have intended by the use of 'Son of man' as a title for himself, it is clear from Synoptic usage that it referred especially (but not exclusively) to his character as the one who should come in the end-time in power and judgment and great glory.

II

FROM GALILEE TO JERUSALEM

2.1-25

Chapter 2 should be read as a unity. It is best understood
if it is taken as a meditation, complete in itself, upon the
work and achievement of the incarnate Lord. It reflects
upon how that work was begun amidst everyday circumstances in Galilee and reached its climax in the crucifixion
and resurrection of Christ in Jerusalem. Its achievement
was nothing less than to bring to an end the religion of
Judaism and to put in its place, as the instrument of God's
purpose for the world, the Christian Church, the body of
Christ, alive from the dead. The means by which this
profound meditation is conveyed is parable. Two stories
are told, one of them perhaps a work of the Evangelist's
own imagination, the other a well known incident from the
Synoptic tradition. The placing side by side of two stories,
one historical and the other not, illustrates very clearly St
John's interest in the truth of history rather than in the
historical details of ' what happened '.

1. a marriage in Cana of Galilee

To what extent this story is founded upon fact we have
no means of knowing, and speculation is profitless. It is
the meaning of the parable of the wedding at Cana that is
all-important. In the OT God is frequently said to have
espoused Israel; and the covenant-making at Sinai is represented as the marriage of Yahweh with Israel his bride
(Isa. 54. 5-7; 62.4 f.; Jer. 2.2; Ezek. 16.8, 43, 60; Hos. 2.7,

etc.). But Israel had been unfaithful and had gone after other gods (Hos. 4.10-15; Ezek. 16.15-43). In the NT the analogy is continued, and Christ is represented as the Bridegroom of a New Israel (Eph. 5.22-33), a figure which appears in Johannine thought (Rev. 19.7-9; 21.2, 9). In the parable of the wedding at Cana, St John is setting forth the Galilean preaching of Jesus as the time of the divine election and espousal of the New Israel, the Church his bride. Christ's work on earth was to call, choose and commission the new instrument of the realization of God's purpose; and strong emphasis is laid upon Jesus' actual *choice* of the disciples (e.g. John 15.16) and upon their actual *union* with him (e.g. 17.21-23; cf. again Eph. 5.22-23). It is a complete mistake, for all that we recognize that St John uses parables of this kind, to think that he is indifferent to the facts of history, since it is the meaning of an historical fact which he is stressing: Jesus's ministry, begun in Galilee, was the day of the espousal of the new Israel, the Church which is one flesh with Christ, united with him in one body (cf. 2.21). This aspect of NT thought is finely expressed in the well-known lines of S. J. Stone's great hymn:

> ' The Church's one foundation
>   Is Jesus Christ her Lord;
> She is his new creation
>   By water and the Word
> From heaven he came and sought her
>   To be his holy Bride,
> With his own Blood he bought her
>   And for her life he died.'

This verse gives wonderful expression to the theology of St John; the fifth and sixth lines express the essential meaning of the parable of the wedding at Cana. Obviously the Evangelist could not represent Jesus as himself the bride-

groom at a village wedding, but by setting Christ forth as
the one who provides the good wine (there is a deep
eucharistic reference here) St John is teaching us that the
earthly ministry of the Lord was the preparation for the
glorious consummation, THE MARRIAGE OF THE LAMB, the
MYSTERY, of which St Paul speaks, IN REGARD OF CHRIST
AND OF THE CHURCH (Eph. 5.32; cf. Rev. 19.7, etc.).

the mother of Jesus

It is tempting to turn the parable into an allegory and
find hidden meanings in every detail. Thus, THE THIRD DAY
might be a cryptic allusion to the resurrection; THE MOTHER
OF JESUS might be a symbol of the faithful remnant of
Israel, which brought forth the Messiah. Some support
for the latter suggestion might be forthcoming from Rev.
12.1-6, 13-17, where some such symbolism is involved. It
would, however, be precarious to adopt such subjective
allegorical interpretations. The remaining references to the
mother of Jesus (who is never named) in the Fourth Gospel
are factual enough (2.12; 6.42, and 19.25-27, though allegorical interpretations have been suggested for the last
of them; see below *ad loc.*). On the whole it seems wiser to
treat the story not as an allegory but as a parable, carrying
one main lesson, and only one.

4. Woman

On English ears this literal translation sounds harsh, as
it would not in the original; cf. 4.21; 19.26. There is no
precise English equivalent of this usage; perhaps ' madam '
comes nearest, but is too cold and distant.

mine hour

This solemn expression concerning Jesus's HOUR occurs
several times (7.30; 8.20; 12.23, 27; 13.1; 17.1; cf. also
Mark 14.35, 41; Luke 22.53; John 16.4); it means the hour
of Christ's crucifixion and resurrection, considered as the

moment of the achievement of the divine purpose of fulfilment and new creation. The transformation of Judaism
cannot be finally accomplished until Christ is crucified,
risen and ascended. Only the beginning of the miracle takes
place in the Galilean ministry (see v. 11).

6. the Jews' manner of purifying

The inadequacy of the Jewish purificatory washings in
water is being contrasted with the cleansing and feasting
which the Church enjoys in the blood of Jesus Christ. In
Johannine thought Christ's blood represents cleansing or
remission of sins (John 1.29; I John 1.7; Rev. 1.5; 7.14),
such a redemption as Jewish cultus could not effect. But it
also represents the very life of God, received by the faithful in the Eucharist (John 6.53-56).

two or three firkins apiece

That there is no symbolical significance in the figures
mentioned in this verse seems all the more probable in
view of the vague TWO OR THREE. Each of the six vessels
must have contained twenty or more gallons. This consideration alone is sufficient to convince us that the story
is a parable, not an actual historical event. To create such
a quantity of good wine WHEN MEN HAVE DRUNK FREELY
(v. 10) would make a poor BEGINNING OF MIRACLES for the
Good Teacher of the Christian tradition. There is, of course,
also the difficulty that the Synoptists know nothing of the
incident. It is easier in every way to understand the story
as a parable, based perhaps upon sayings of Jesus which
liken his teaching to new wine which would burst the out-
moded forms of Judaism (e.g. Mark 2.22; Luke 5.39).

9. the servants which had drawn the water knew

The whole Bible teaches that the knowledge of God
comes by obedience to his will, and this is a truth which
St John strongly emphasizes (e.g. 7.17).

11. This beginning of his signs

The historical truth is that the process of changing the water of Judaism into the GOOD WINE of Christ began with the ministry of Jesus in Galilee, but it was not completed until the Lord's earthly ministry was consummated by his triumphant death in Jerusalem. We have no knowledge at all why St John associates the opening of the ministry with Cana, and we cannot even conjecture why he stresses the point so heavily (cf. also 4.46). Cana does not figure in the Synoptic tradition and indeed is not mentioned in the Bible outside the Fourth Gospel.

NOTE ON 'SIGNS' IN THE FOURTH GOSPEL

The word 'sign' (Gk. *sēmeion*) occurs seventeen times in St John's Gospel and bears a weighty meaning. It is used of the mighty works of Jesus, which St John never calls miracles (Gk. *dunameis*) or wonders (Gk. *terata*) (except perhaps once in a deprecatory way at 4.48, his only use of the word). By the use of the word 'signs' St. John indicates that the miracles of the Lord are enacted parables, whose deep significance cannot be perceived except by the eyes of faith. In this matter he is in complete agreement with the Synoptists; he merely underlines the implicit teaching of St Mark, and he introduces no new motives into the telling of miracle-stories. There is no specifically Johannine interpretation of the miracles of Jesus. St John agrees with the Synoptists that they have a deep spiritual meaning and that this meaning has nothing to do with their impressiveness as wonders (2.18; 4.48; 6.26, 30; 20.29). Yet the miracles recounted in the Fourth Gospel are all of them very great supernatural acts of power: they were not the kind of 'wonders' which any village sorcerer might work, or the symbolic actions which any prophet in Israel might have performed. They were 'the works which none other did'

(15.24). But their meaning is known only to those who have faith in Christ, and in several cases a miracle is used as the peg or 'text' on which to hang a long discourse of the Lord's. Thus, the Feeding Miracle of 6.4-13 becomes the occasion of the discourse upon the significance of the Eucharist in the Church in 6.26-65. It is true to say that these discourses are only an elucidation of the meaning which is already implicit in those miracles that have a parallel in St Mark. Seven 'signs' are recounted in the Fourth Gospel: the Changing of the Water into Wine (2.1-11); the Healing of the Nobleman's Son (4.46-54); the Healing of the Impotent man (5.2-9); the Feeding of the Five Thousand (6.4-13); the Walking on the Water (6. 16-21); the Healing of the Man Born Blind (9.1-7), and the Raising of Lazarus (11.1-44). Of these only the first and the last have no parallel in the Synoptists. The number seven may be symbolic of the perfection of the revelation given through the deeds of the Lord; St John, of course, is aware that Jesus worked many other signs besides these seven (20.30; 21.25). Apart from faith in Christ the signs have no meaning; there were many who saw the signs with their outward eyes and yet did not believe (12.37). If we believe that Jesus Christ is truly the Son of God, then we shall understand the mighty works which he wrought; they will no longer be stumbling-blocks to us or mere meaningless wonders; the hidden glory of the Lord shines through them to those disciples who believe on him (cf. 2.11). And St John speaks a personal word to us on the question of the miracles of Jesus: BLESSED ARE THEY THAT HAVE NOT SEEN, AND YET HAVE BELIEVED (20.29).

12. Capernaum

St John now briefly alludes to that part of the Synoptic tradition which deals with the short period (NOT MANY DAYS) when Jesus's ministry was centred upon Capernaum (Matt. 4.13; Mark 1.21; 2.1; Luke 4.23).

13. Jesus went up to Jerusalem

According to the Synoptic tradition, when the Galilean ministry was over, Jesus went up to Jerusalem, where, during the week which began with the Cleansing of the Temple, he taught publicly for a day or two, kept the passover feast with his disciples on the Thursday evening, was arrested and tried during that night, condemned on the Friday morning, crucified at noon the same day and buried in the late afternoon; very early on the following Sunday morning his tomb was found empty, and afterwards he appeared to his disciples. St John does not wish to alter this tradition. He is meditating upon its significance. He is not providing an alternative history of the life of Jesus in which the Cleansing of the Temple takes place not at the end but at the beginning of his ministry. The visit to Jerusalem to which this verse refers is the same visit—in Passion Week—as that which St Mark describes (11.1-18). The whole of this second chapter of St John constitutes a unity, as we have said, and it forms a meditation upon the Synoptic record of the life, death and resurrection of Jesus. That record, St John is telling us, is the story of the divine rejection of the Jews and of the abolition of Judaism. The work begun in Galilee is completed in Jerusalem. Instead of the Temple, which was to be destroyed, the new Temple of Christ's body was to be the place where God henceforward should be known and adored, the universal Church of Jesus Christ (cf. 4.21-24). We need not suppose that St John was in possession of a chronology of the ministry that was independent of St Mark's or that he is giving us evidence of an earlier visit to Jerusalem than the one which St Mark mentions. His aim is to demonstrate the truth of the Synoptic history, and this he does by setting forth in outline the whole earthly ministry of Jesus as in itself a kind of 'sign'—a story with a profound meaning.

14. those that sold oxen

Pilgrims from the whole Jewish Dispersion as well as from Palestine came to keep the passover in Jerusalem in accordance with the prescription of the Law (Deut. 16.5 f.; cf. Ex. 12.14-20; Lev. 23.5). It was more convenient to buy oxen, etc., for sacrifices than to bring them perhaps hundreds of miles. The money changers exchanged the various foreign currencies of the pilgrims for the Temple currency (with which alone the oxen, etc., could be bought) at a very high rate of profit.

15. a scourge of cords

This detail is not mentioned in the Synoptic accounts (Matt. 21.12-17; Mark 11.15-18; Luke 19.45 f.). It is beloved of anti-pacifists, but it hardly proves that Jesus succeeded in driving out the marketeers by physical violence rather than by moral force; the whip was doubtless a symbol of authority. None of the Evangelists is interested in such questions; they do not tell us how large was the body of Jesus's supporters, because they consider such matters irrelevant to the meaning of the event. That meaning, of course, is the pronouncing of God's judgment upon faithless Judaism and its Temple.

17. The zeal of thine house

The quotation is apposite because the Psalmist is saying that the reproach which he bears is due to his zeal for God's house (Ps. 69.9).

What sign shewest thou . . . ?

The demand for signs of one's own choosing, involving the rejection of the signs which God has actually vouchsafed, is sternly condemned in the Bible (Ex. 4.1, 8; 7.9, etc.); to demand a sign is to tempt God (Ps. 95.9). Cf. also Mark 8.11 f.; Matt. 16.1-4; John 6.30.

C

19. Destroy this Temple

The Synoptists record this saying as one of the accusations brought against Jesus at his trial (Mark 14.58; cf. 15.29), and the fact that St John introduces it at this point confirms the view that he is now meditating upon the conclusion of Christ's ministry, not its beginning. Jesus taught that the Temple, whose destruction he predicted (Mark 13.2; Luke 19.41-44), was to be replaced by the new Temple of the Church which he would build (Matt. 16.18). St John, who would be thoroughly familiar with St Paul's teaching about the Church as the body of Christ, correctly interprets the intention of Jesus: HE SPAKE OF THE TEMPLE OF HIS BODY. The three days, of course, refers to the traditional period which Christ lay in the tomb: Jewish reckoning included the Friday and the Sunday as whole days.

20. Forty and six years

The re-building of the Temple by Herod the Great, to which this passage refers, was begun in 20 BC; if we add 46 years to this date, we are brought down to about 27 BC, which is not bad reckoning by ancient standards. In fact, the re-building was not finished until AD 63. In AD 70 the Temple was utterly destroyed by the Romans.

22. his disciples remembered

St. John makes it clear that it was not until after Christ's resurrection that the disciples came to understand what he had said and done (cf. 12.16; 13.7); it was the guidance of the Holy Spirit that led them into the truth (14.26; 16.13).

they believed the scripture

That is, they believed the scriptural testimony concerning the resurrection of Christ (e.g. Ps. 16.10); cf. John 20.9; Luke 24.46.

23. beholding his signs

Conclusive evidence is here provided that St John refers to the events of Passiontide (and not to a Cleansing of the Temple at the beginning of the ministry) by this reference to 'signs'; in 4.54 he tells us that Jesus's second 'sign' was the Healing of the Nobleman's Son at Capernaum. In short, St John is not arranging his Gospel in a chronological order at all.

24. Although during Passion Week Jesus at first had many adherents, such as those who supported him when he drove out the money-changers, he did not trust himself to them and withdrew to the safety of a nearby village every evening (Mark 11.19).

III

BAPTISMAL REGENERATION

3.1-36

St John's method of presenting the truth concerning Christ is often to cast his teaching into the form of a discourse between Jesus and some enquirer or of a controversy between Jesus and 'the Jews'. The teaching thus given is clearly a meditation upon certain aspects of Christ's words and works as recorded in the Synoptic tradition. It is usually a development of what is already implicit in the Synoptists, and it represents the Church's reflection upon the Gospel tradition at the end of the first century AD. How far the actual words of the historical Jesus are preserved in the Johannine discourses it is impossible to say, and different readers of the Gospels will make different estimates. The theme of Chapter 3 is the meaning of Christian Baptism and its connection with Judgment, and there are appended some further reflections upon the mission and witness of John the Baptist. St John believes that the Holy Spirit has enlightened the mind of the apostolic Church so that it understands, as the disciples before the crucifixion could not have understood, what is the true meaning of the actions and words of the Jesus of history. He puts into the mouth of the historical Jesus the teaching which the Spirit of the Risen Christ had given to the apostolic Church through the prophets (see 12.16; 13.7; 14.26; 15.26; 16.12 f.; Rev. 2.7, 11, 17, 29; 3.6, 13, 22; 13.9). Thus in the conversation with Nicodemus the necessity of Christian Baptism is affirmed. The Church since the apostolic age has understood Jesus to have taught that salvation is appropriated by the individual through baptism into the Church, his resurrection body; St John is here asserting this catholic and apostolic doctrine. He does not use the word 'baptism', doubtless because in his day Christians were very reluctant to speak of their 'mysteries' in documents which might fall into the hands of pagans or of the Roman government officials. As the Apocalypse vividly reminds us, the latter were avid to punish and suppress any religion for which Caesar was not King of kings and Lord of lords. The Christian mysteries had to be celebrated in desert places or behind locked doors. But now it is Nicodemus who comes to Jesus secretly.

1. a man of the Pharisees

The Pharisees constituted the large popular party within Judaism, distinguished alike from the aristocratic Sadducean minority, which depended on Roman support, and from the fanatical Zealot revolutionaries of the left. The rabbis met with up and down Palestine belonged to this party, with its strict devotion to the due observance of the Law. It is implied that Nicodemus was a rabbi of some status (v. 10); we should think of him as being in the same class as Gamaliel.

Nicodemus

The name is Greek but it had been adopted by the Jews in the form 'Naqdimon'. It means 'conqueror of the people'. If Nicodemus is not a real historical person but only a literary device of the Evangelist's, the name would be suitable as suggesting authority. There is no means of identifying him with any known historical figure in Jerusalem in the time of our Lord.

a ruler of the Jews

Probably this means a member of the Sanhedrin, the

puppet government which the Romans allowed the Jews to maintain. Since its seventy members were mostly Sadducees, there was little likelihood of its incurring the displeasure of the Romans. A few outstanding Pharisaic doctors of the Law were members of it (cf. Acts 5.34: Gamaliel was, of course, a Pharisee).

2. by night

Night and darkness have deep symbolical significance in the Fourth Gospel (cf. 1.5; 3.19; 13.30). Historically the situation is well founded; a distinguished doctor of the Law could hardly be seen conversing with the disreputable carpenter-rabbi from Galilee.

no man can do these signs

As we have pointed out, St John is not interested in chronological development; the SECOND SIGN THAT JESUS DID is not recorded until much later (see 4.54).

3. Except a man be born anew

The Greek word for ' anew ' can also mean ' from above ' (RV marg.), and St John is deliberately ambiguous and intends both meanings. Regeneration (a Latin word meaning ' being born again ') is a necessary condition of entry into the reign of God. It is explained in v. 5 that this means being ' born of water and the Spirit ', i.e., Christian baptism, which is, of course, re-birth into the new life through the gift of the Holy Spirit; it is entry into the Church, the family of God's children (see on 1.13), the body of Christ, the place where God reigns on earth (THE KINGDOM OF GOD).

he cannot see the kingdom of God

This phrase is explained in v. 5 as meaning CANNOT ENTER INTO THE KINGDOM OF GOD. St John only here uses the frequent Synoptic phrase, KINGDOM OF GOD; he uses LIFE or ETERNAL LIFE as a synonym for it. St Mark himself has done the same thing (Mark 9.43 and 45 compared with v. 47), and thus the usage is not peculiarly Johannine. The Kingdom (better, reign) of God, or eternal life, is that gift of salvation at the end of history, when God's purpose is consummated, which all devout Jews long to obtain (e.g. Matt. 25.34; Mark 10.17; John 5.39). Christian baptism, the entry into the sphere of the outpoured Spirit of the end-time, is already, as it were, an entry into the reign of God which shall be manifested at Christ's return in glory; it is even now by faith an anticipation of the life of the age to come.

4. Nicodemus's gauche question is characteristic of St John's technique; the questioner misunderstands what Christ has said, so that he is given the opportunity of fuller explanation (e.g. 4.11; 6.52; 14.5, 8, etc.).

6. There is a fuller discussion of flesh and spirit in 6.52-63, and it is expedient to withold comment until then.

8. The wind bloweth where it listeth
The double meaning of St John's Greek cannot here be translated. Since *pneuma* means 'wind', 'breath' or 'spirit', the following meaning is also implied: 'The Spirit breathes where he wills.' The point is that the workings of the divine Spirit are utterly beyond the comprehension or prediction of our human reason. The baptized (those BORN OF THE SPIRIT, cf. I Cor. 12.13) are caught up into the supernatural sphere of the Spirit's operation.

10. A learned teacher of the Law should have known these things, because they are all contained in the Scriptures.

12. Perhaps the verse means that if Nicodemus does not understand teaching conveyed under the form of parables of nature—birth, the blowing of the wind—he is unlikely to understand if Jesus speaks directly of heavenly things without the use of parables.

13. And no man hath ascended into heaven

That is, to discover truth directly on behalf of the human race (cf. Deut. 30.12; Prov. 30.4); it is axiomatic with the biblical writers that there is no mystic flight of the soul into the heavenly regions by which mankind might know the truth of God. Such truth is knowable only in so far as God has willed to reveal it. There is no true knowledge of God save through the Word, which was in the beginning with God, and which now has come down from heaven and tabernacles in the person of the Son of Man—that is, in human form—and will ascend again into heaven. The actual words used by St John imply that the Son of Man has already ascended into heaven, but of course St John is writing from the standpoint of the Spirit-filled Church after the ascension of Christ.

14. And as Moses lifted up the serpent

According to the story in Num. 21.4-9 the plague of fiery serpents was stayed when Moses made a brazen serpent and set it on a standard: IT CAME TO PASS, THAT IF A SERPENT HAD BITTEN ANY MAN, WHEN HE LOOKED UNTO THE SERPENT OF BRASS, HE LIVED. For St John this is a parable of Jesus and his cross. Before the Son of Man could ascend into heaven, he must first suffer and die (cf. the Synoptic THE SON OF MAN MUST SUFFER, Mark 8.31, etc.; Luke 24.7). This was the only means by which men could be saved from the power of the Serpent—a symbolical figure in the Johannine theology (cf. Rev. 12.9; 20.2, and cf. also Gen. 3.1); by looking in faith upon the Son of Man on his cross, mankind could be saved (v. 15). It is characteristic of the thinking of St John that the suffering and triumph of Christ are not two things but one; the victorious Lion of the tribe of Judah is also the Lamb standing as though he had been slain (Rev. 5.5 f.). The exaltation of Christ is his crucifixion; the cross is the throne of the King of Israel. The expression 'lifting up' ('exaltation') becomes in the Fourth Gospel a technical expression for the crucifixion (8.28; 12.32, 34). The crucifixion is the hour of Christ's glorification (7.39; 12.16, 23; 13.31 f.; 17.1).

15. eternal life

This expression occurs very frequently in St John. Sometimes, however, he speaks simply of LIFE without the adjective (e.g. 10.10); but the meaning is the same, namely, the life of the age to come. The concept is synonymous with the Synoptic figure of the Kingdom of God (see note on 3.3 above). It has nothing whatever to do with Platonic notions of life of a 'timeless' quality, which are quite foreign to Hebrew thinking. It is the life of the blessed in the world to come, when God has brought history to its consummation, the life which can be spoken of only in figures, such as those found in Rev. 19.6-9; 21.1-6, 10-27; 22.1-5. The meaning of 'life' in St John can be expressed by saying that it is an eschatological conception; it means life in the end-time, a life which may be known by faith even now by those who have recognized in the coming of the Word made flesh the opening act of the drama of the divine consummation of history.

16. God so loved the world

This great affirmation shews us that, although THE WORLD is alienated from God, he has not abandoned it. His unmerited love—*agapē* in the NT means the love even of that which is unlovable and repulsive—is the ground of the incarnation; the verb used here is the cognate of the noun *agapē*, which is to be contrasted with *ĕrōs*, the love that is evoked by the attractiveness of its object. *Eros* nowhere occurs in the NT. For the meaning of 'world' in St John see note on 1.10.

17. God sent not the Son . . . to judge the world

St John in this passage is teaching that the object of
the incarnation was the salvation of the world, not its condemnation. But the coming of the light inevitably involved
judgment, though this was not its purpose, because light
' shews up ' all defects and blemishes. Moreover, sinful men
do not love the light; they prefer the darkness which cloaks
their wickedness. Burglars prefer to work by night (vv. 19 f.).
St John does not share the optimism concerning human
nature of Tennyson and the Victorians that ' we needs
must love the highest when we see it '.

saved through him

St John speaks of Christ as the Saviour of the world; see
note on 4.42 below, and cf. 12.47; I John 4.14.

18. hath been judged already

It is sometimes said that in the Fourth Gospel there is
no last judgment and that the only judgment is that which
takes place now in this life; a man is judged by his response
to Christ and in this way he may be said to judge himself.
All such notions are contrary to the clear statements of the
Evangelist; see 5.22-29 and the notes on this passage below.
St John here means that the man who believes is not
condemned or judged adversely; this is his way of stating
the truth which is sometimes spoken of as the Pauline
doctrine of justification by faith. But it would be better to
speak of St Paul's doctrine of baptismal justification, because St Paul thinks of baptism as the death (richly
deserved) of the sinner, from which he arises to the life in
Christ, which is already through the gift of the Spirit the
earnest or foretaste of the life of the age to come (Rom.
6.3-7). Baptism is judgment, but it does not result in condemnation because of belief in Jesus Christ, with whom
the baptized are united in one body; St Paul and St John
are agreed that the new life of the faithful is the result of

their union with Christ. St. John, unlike St Paul, does not stress baptism as a dying; but the idea is implicit when he makes the Baptist speak of THE LAMB OF GOD WHICH TAKETH AWAY THE SIN OF THE WORLD (1.29). Though for the reasons we have noted he does not mention the baptism of Jesus, he is well aware that Jesus's baptism was a bearing of the sins of the world and as such a pre-figuring of his death upon the cross. For Christians the day of their baptism is in an important sense their judgment day, and they are not condemned. But neither St. Paul nor St John thinks that this means that there will be no final day of judgment. For Christians, however, it will be the day of joyful resurrection (cf. John 6.40, 54). The fundamental meaning of 'eternal life' in St. John is the life to which believers are raised up at the last day: THIS IS THE WILL OF MY FATHER, THAT EVERY ONE THAT BEHOLDETH THE SON, AND BELIEVETH ON HIM, SHOULD HAVE ETERNAL LIFE, THAT I SHOULD RAISE HIM UP ON THE LAST DAY (John 6.40, RV marg.).

21. he that doeth the truth

This very biblical and Hebraic phrase indicates a totally different conception of truth from that of the Greeks, for whom the truth was supremely the object of intellectual contemplation (*theoria*). For the Hebrew truth is something to be done; it is known only by obedience to the will of God; cf. 2.9 (and note above); 3.36; 7.17. To do the truth means to practise the Christian faith and this can only be done through divine grace (WROUGHT IN GOD).

22.

The baptismal theme which pervades this chapter seems to have prompted further reflections upon the witness of John the Baptist. It is impossible to make historical or even chronological sense of this passage, and all attempts to re-arrange the order of St John's narrative are unconvincing. We are told that Jesus now came into Judaea, but we have never been told that he had left it, since Jerusalem was the last place mentioned (2.23). But, as we have said, St. John is not attempting to write in chronological sequence. The statement that Jesus baptized as a rival practitioner to the Baptist (cf. v. 24), both in v. 22 and in v. 26, cannot be reconciled with the Synoptic narratives, in which the public ministry of Jesus did not begin until after John had been imprisoned by Herod (Mark 1.14). Further confusion is created by John 4.1 f., where it seems as if someone has attempted half-heartedly to correct the statement that Jesus himself baptized: it was only his disciples who baptized converts. But it is incredible on all grounds that there should have been any Christian baptism before the ascension of Christ, but chiefly on the ground stated by St John himself in 7.39: THE SPIRIT WAS NOT YET GIVEN, BECAUSE JESUS WAS NOT YET GLORIFIED. Christian baptism was essentially baptism in Holy Spirit (John 1.33; Mark 1.8; Acts 1.5). How then can we explain these difficulties? They can be explained only by recognizing the true character of St John's Gospel: it does not purport to give a rival history and chronology to those of the Synoptists: it frankly reads the historical issues of St John's own times back into the story of Jesus and his ministry. The historical situation at the end of the first century was that in various parts of the world, including Ephesus (Acts 19.1-7), the disciples of John the Baptist were administering a rival baptism to that of Christ. The testimony of the Baptist that he is not the Messiah but only the one sent before him (v. 28) is repeated from 1.20-23, and the Baptist is made to declare that his followers must decrease while those of Christ increase (v.30).

29. He that hath the bride

Christ is the Bridegroom whose bride is Israel (see note on 2.1 above); the Baptist is only the friend of the Bridegroom or, as we would say, the 'best man' at the wedding.

This metaphor confirms the interpretation of the story of the Marriage at Cana, which we have given above.

31. The character of St John's writing in this chapter is well illustrated by the fact that any reference to who is the speaker in vv. 31-6 has been omitted. Presumably Christ, not the Baptist, is now speaking. What we have in fact is, of course, the Spirit-inspired meditation of the Evangelist himself. The meaning of v. 31 is that Christ comes FROM ABOVE, while John the Baptist is a purely human (EARTHLY) figure; hence Christ's baptism is FROM ABOVE (3.3, 5, RV marg.), while John's is of this world.

32. Cf. 3.11; 8.14, 26; also, for the second half of the verse, 1.11; 3.19; 5.43; 12.37.

34. It is repeated several times and in different ways in the Fourth Gospel that Christ is God's emissary, that he speaks the words of God and works the works of God. The Spirit ABODE upon Jesus (1.32), and it abode upon him in full measure.

36. see life

That is, ' enter into the life of the age to come '; cf. SEE THE KINGDOM OF GOD, ENTER INTO THE KINGDOM OF GOD, 3.3, 5.

the wrath of God

This is the only mention of wrath in the Fourth Gospel, but the theme occurs frequently in the Apocalypse (cf. Rev. 6.16, THE WRATH OF THE LAMB). It is a logical correlate of the idea of judgment, and it expresses in a necessarily anthropomorphic way the reaction of the righteous God to the disobedient unbelievers who reject the light. In the NT generally ' wrath ' is an eschatological conception (cf. Rom. 2.5; Rev. 6.17), as indeed it is here.

IV

THE UNIVERSAL GOSPEL

4.1-42

St John was writing in an age in which the promised pouring out of the Spirit UPON ALL FLESH (Joel 2.28) had been abundantly fulfilled, and when there were Spirit-endowed churches of Jesus Christ all over the known world (cf. Rev. 2.7, etc.; 7.9). A mission to the whole world is implicit in the Synoptic tradition, and indeed St Mark, who gathered that tradition into the earliest known Gospel, had spent a lifetime as a missionary of the faith and in all probability wrote his book in Rome itself. But there are few words of the Lord, even in St Mark's Gospel, which refer directly to a mission of the Church to the Gentiles (there is, however, Mark 13.10; cf. Matt. 28.19; Luke 24.47). It is natural that St John should meditate upon the universal character of the Gospel of Christ, and it is characteristic of his method that he should cast his meditation into the form of a dialogue between Jesus and a Samaritan woman. He well knew that Jesus himself had not preached directly to the Gentiles. In 12.20 f. he records the request of certain Greeks to see Jesus, but he does not tell us whether their request was granted. But, as the Synoptists record, Jesus had to travel through Samaria in order to pass between Galilee and Judaea; and thus a conversation with a Samaritan would by no means be historically improbable. We have no means of telling whether the episode at Sychar is founded on fact or which if any of the words of the conversation with the Samaritan woman were actually spoken by the historical Jesus. That he should have declared openly that he was the Messiah on such an occasion (4.26) must be declared improbable, if the Synoptic tradition itself is reliable. It is therefore wiser to regard the conversation as a meditation on the theme of the universality of the Gospel, composed by the Evangelist himself in the light of his reflection upon the activity of the Holy Spirit in the world-wide Church. Again, he is concerned with the meaning of history rather than with the literal writing of it. Of course, the content of this wonderful dialogue is divinely inspired revelation, for St John, as he would claim, is guided by the Spirit of God to understand the significance of the words and works of the Jesus of history. When the Church was led by the Spirit to include St John's Gospel in the canon of her sacred Scriptures, the interpretation of history which that Evangelist gives us was endorsed as being the divinely illumined expression of the truth of history.

4. Samaria

Samaria, a region politically joined with Judaea under direct Roman rule, west of the Jordan, bounded by Galilee and Judaea on the north and south respectively, now constituted a half-foreign population dividing the Jews of those two lands from one another. Pilgrims from Galilee on their way to Jerusalem had to pass through Samaria unless they made a detour east of Jordan (cf. Luke 9.52). When in 721 B.C. the cream of the population of the Northern Kingdom of Israel ('the ten tribes'), whose capital was at Samaria, was deported by the Assyrians (cf. II Kings 17.6; 18.11), the foreigners who were settled in their place desired to practise the cultus of the 'god' of the land (II Kings 17.24-41); but they were ostracized by the Jews of Judaea and allowed no part in the worship of the Temple in Jerusalem (Neh. 4.1 f.; 13.23-31). The Samaritans, thus repulsed, observed their own cultus, modelled on the Pentateuch, which was their sacred book, and offered their sacrifices upon

Mount Gerizim, their sacred mountain; and to this century a handful of them has survived in this place, observing their ancient religious practices in the traditional way. Thus, though the Samaritans regarded themselves as true worshippers of Yahweh, Israel's God, the Jews had no dealings with them and treated them as unclean foreigners. Hence a conversation with a Samaritan offers St John an appropriate occasion for a consideration of the universal character of the Christian faith as contrasted with Jewish exclusiveness. One aspect of the truth of history which St John underlines is provided with a factual basis in St Luke's Gospel, where the favourable attitude of Jesus towards the Samaritans is illustrated by his story about a *good* Samaritan (Luke 10.33) and by his commendation of a *grateful* Samaritan (17.16).

6. Jacob's well

The significance of this detail appears in v. 12: Jacob, the old Israel, gave a well of natural water, and those who drink of it cannot find permanent satisfaction in it; Jesus is the new Israel, who provides a well-spring of living (i.e. life-giving) water, which alone can eternally satisfy the spiritual needs of men's souls (v. 14). (As RV marg. points out, different Greek words are used for 'well' in the passage.)

about the sixth hour

That is, about midday.

9. a Samaritan woman

That a Jew would speak with a Samaritan was, if anything, rather less surprising than that a rabbi would speak with a woman. Judaism is the most masculine of all the world's religions; a Jew thanked God daily that he was not born a woman, and the rabbis used to debate whether women had souls. Women had almost no civil rights (e.g.

in the matter of divorce) and took almost no part in religious ceremonies; in the Temple they were not allowed beyond the Court of Women. It is St Luke, who notes Jesus's sympathy with the despised Samaritans, who also records his sympathy with the despised sex. The revolution accomplished in the matter of the status of women by the teaching and example of Jesus is hardly ever recognized for what indeed it is, namely, one of the most important social advances in the history of civilization. If we have any historical imagination at all, we should be able to perceive something of the magnitude of the conversion which had been wrought in the heart of a pupil of Gamaliel's who could actually write that IN CHRIST THERE CAN BE NEITHER MALE NOR FEMALE (Gal. 3.28).

Jews have no dealings with Samaritans

This clause was probably added by an early copyist to explain the situation for the benefit of readers who did not know Palestine; it is not found in some of the oldest MSS (see RV marg.).

10. living water

In a dry land water is not taken for granted, as it is in a western city where we need only turn a tap; it is a boon of incomparable value. Hence the biblical metaphor of water is not so easily appreciated by us to-day. The phrase LIVING WATERS is found in Jer. 2.13, where it implies that God himself is the perennial fountain of the true life of Israel; also in Jer. 17.13. For the use of the phrase in the natural sense of life-giving water see Gen. 26.19 (RV marg.). Other OT passages which might be noted for the biblical sense of the metaphor include Ps. 42.1 f.; Isa. 43.20; 44.3; 55.1; Ezek. 47.1 (cf. Rev. 22.1); Zech. 14.8. The Johannine conception of LIVING WATER or THE WATER OF LIFE reappears in John 7.37 f., and in Rev. 21.6 and 22.17. The rabbis had identified the water of life with the Torah; St

John declares that the life-giving water is to be found not in the Torah but in Christ (cf. John 5.39); those who drink of the Torah thirst again. The well of Torah is deep and much fetching and carrying are required; a great sum of labour must be paid. But Jesus dispenses of the GIFT OF GOD (v. 10) without price: I WILL GIVE UNTO HIM THAT IS ATHIRST OF THE FOUNTAIN OF THE WATER OF LIFE *FREELY* (Rev. 21.6). The eschatological sense of 'life' is, of course, here as everywhere retained; cf. v. 14, THE WATER THAT I SHALL GIVE HIM SHALL BECOME IN HIM A WELL OF WATER SPRING-ING UP UNTO THE LIFE OF THE WORLD TO COME.

18. thou hast had five husbands
Another example of St John's belief that Jesus possessed a supernatural knowledge concerning other people; see note on 1.47 above. The suggestion that the woman represents Samaria and the five husbands represent the various false gods whom the Samaritans had worshipped (cf. II Kings 17.33-41) is not very convincing; St John deals in parables, not allegories, Such plausibility as it possesses is derived from the biblical metaphor of the nation or tribe as being 'espoused' to its own particular god; polytheism is poly-gamy; see note on 2.1 above.

20. this mountain
That is, Mount Gerizim. The Deuteronomic legislators had decreed that sacrifice could be offered to Yahweh only in one sanctuary (Deut. 12.5; 16.2; 26.2), which for the Jews was, of course, Mount Zion in Jerusalem. Excluded from Zion, the Samaritans said that the 'one place' of worship was Mount Gerizim, and they could find Penta-teuchal evidence for their claim (Deut. 11.29; 27.12).

ye say
That is, 'you Jews say'.

21. The meaning is that 'you Samaritans, after your con-

version, will worship according to neither the Jerusalem nor the Gerizim cultus.' The evangelization of the Samaritans is described in Acts 8.4-25.

22. Salvation is from the Jews

Despite his antipathy to 'the Jews', St John well knows that the Jews, and not the Samaritans or any other nation, were historically the chosen instrument by which God had in the past worked out his plan for the salvation of the world. Thus, there was a difference between the worship of the Jews and that of the Samaritans; the former possessed a certain knowledge of what they were doing, while the Samaritans ignorantly worshipped the great Unknown, like the Athenians of Mars Hill (Acts 17.23).

23. The hour cometh, and now is

This means, 'The time is near, and indeed with the coming of the Messiah has actually arrived, when . . .' What we have called the 'end-time', the last or Messianic period of cosmic history, has now dawned. This is the consistent Johannine point of view; cf. I John 2.18, LITTLE CHILDREN, IT IS THE LAST HOUR. Cf. also John 5.25. The characteristic of this last age of world history will be the worshipping Church, the universal community of the Messiah, itself the sign of the End.

in spirit and truth

Here 'spirit' should be written with a capital letter. THE SPIRIT OF TRUTH is a characteristically Johannine designation of the Holy Spirit (John 14.17; 15.26; 16.13). The difference between Christian worship and that of the Jews and Samaritans was that the former was Spirit-inspired; the whole life of the Messianic community of the latter days was permeated by the outpoured Spirit of the end-time (cf. Rom. 8.15; Eph. 6.18, etc; cf. Zech. 12.10, I WILL POUR . . . THE SPIRIT OF SUPPLICATION).

such doth the Father seek

The NT (and indeed the whole Bible) emphasizes the divine initiative in the search for man's soul (e.g. Luke 15.3-10). ' Religion ' is not man's search for God, but God's search for man : Christ is the Good Shepherd (John 10.11), but it is the Father who draws men to Christ (John 6.44). Our ' religion ' may feel like *our* search for God, but in reality it is only our *response* to the God who is searching for us (cf. I John 4.19; Rev. 3.20).

24. God is Spirit

So we should translate (with RV marg.). If a Greek philosopher had said this, or even a Platonizing Jew like Philo, he would have meant that God was incorporeal, transcendent, super-rational, non-anthropomorphic, and so on. But St John is not arguing for the existence of the Supreme Being of Greek philosophy. ' Spirit ' in the Bible (and in St John) is the life-giving breath of God (cf. Gen. 2.7), which quickens and illumines the hearts and minds of men. It is God who gives the Spirit, who indeed is one with the Spirit, in the same way that he is one with his own creative Word (John 1.1). When the Spirit of God was outpoured in the latter days, God was giving himself, his own life and breath and power. It is with God's own life, breath and power that God must be worshipped in the Church upon which the Spirit of God has been outpoured. This is the only true or *real* worship (' truth ' means ' reality '). It is God who gives to the Church the power to worship him aright (IN TRUTH).

34. My meat is to do the will

Cf. the quotation of Jesus (in answer to the Devil at the Temptation) of Deut. 8.3, ' Man doth not live by bread only, but by everything that proceedeth out of the mouth of the LORD doth man live ' (i.e. by obedience to God's commands) (Matt. 4.4; Luke 4.4). St John strongly emphasizes the absolute obedience of Jesus to the will of God and his fulfilment of the 'works' of God (5.36; 6.38; 8.29; 9.4; 10.37 f.; 17.4, etc.).

him that sent me

The 'mission' or sending of the Son by the Father is one of the constant themes of the Johannine writings. Some such expression as HIM THAT SENT ME occurs over a score of times in the Gospel; cf. I John 4.14 ,'the Father hath sent the Son to be the Saviour of the world'; cf. also John 3.17.

35. white already unto harvest

The Synoptic tradition records various sayings of the Lord concerning his own mission as a sowing or a reaping (e.g. Mark 4.1-32). St John here makes use of a similar metaphor. Proverbially there are four months between sowing and reaping (in the hot climate of Palestine), but in the case of his own mission sowing and reaping are virtually one process. His disciples' task is to reap the harvest of souls which is already ripe (cf. v. 39). The Q saying about the harvest being plenteous and the labourers few (Matt. 9.37; Luke 10.2) probably supplies the basis of St John's meditation here. The Gospel-preaching is the harvesting of of the labours of all the prophets and wise men of the old dispensation; the age of the Messiah is the age of fulfilment, and the harvest of souls is being reaped. St John is thinking especially of the harvesting that had been accomplished by the Church in Samaria (cf. the 'mission' of St Philip the Evangelist, Acts 8.4-25, which is anticipated, as it were, in vv. 39-42).

39. many of the Samaritans believed

The Synoptic records certainly do not create the impression that Jesus accomplished a successful mission in Samaria (cf. Luke 9.53). But, as we have seen, it is not St

John's purpose to give us an historically and chronologically accurate record of the ministry of Jesus. He is again
at this point in his usual manner reading back into the
historical life of Jesus events which happened after the
resurrection—in this case, the successful evangelization of
Samaria. It was *then* that the Samaritans believed in Christ
—not because they were told about him by a third party,
but because they had encountered the risen Christ in their
own experience and had discovered for themselves that he
was indeed the Saviour of the world (v. 42).

42. the Saviour of the world

In the OT (especially in Deutero-Isaiah) it is the
righteousness of God which accomplishes salvation: Israel
has been disobedient and broken the Covenant; yet Yahweh
remains faithful to his promise and for his righteousness'
sake will accomplish the salvation of his people (cf. Isa.
45.21: A JUST GOD AND A SAVIOUR; cf. also 43.24-26; 44.
2 f.; Deut. 9.5; Ezek. 36.22, 32). The act of creation itself is
poetically depicted as an act of salvation, in which the
world is delivered from the power of the Dragon of Chaos;
and likewise the deliverance of Israel at the Red Sea is
set forth as an act of new creation (Isa. 43.15-19; cf. Ps.
74.12-14; Wisd. 19.6-8). These acts of creation-salvation,
however, are but the foreshadowing of the great deliverance
of the end-time, when God will create new heavens and
a new earth (Isa. 65.17; 66.22; cf. Rev. 21.1, 5). In that day
'all flesh' shall come to worship before the Lord (Isa.
66.23), a prophecy singularly relevant to the theme of St
John's dialogue with the Woman of Samaria. The converted
Samaritans are the harvest of the new creation, of which
the Church of Jesus Christ itself is the first-fruits. St John,
having set forth Christ as the Word or instrument of God,
alike in the first creation and in the new creation of the
end-time, now declares that he is therefore THE SAVIOUR
OF THE WORLD, for it is he by whom the new act of creation-

salvation is being accomplished. The expression occurs again in the NT only at I John 4.14; but cf. John 3.17 and 12.47; also I Tim. 4.10.

THE HEALING OF THE NATIONS

4.43-54

The Book of Acts traces the progress of the Christian faith from Jerusalem through Samaria and on to the Gentile world: ON THE GENTILES ALSO WAS POURED THE GIFT OF THE HOLY SPIRIT (Acts 10.45). It is a striking fact that 'the Pentecost of the Gentiles' should have taken place in the household of a Roman army-officer (Cornelius, the centurion, Acts 10.22). St John likewise traces the flow of the blessings of Christ from Jerusalem to the Samaritans and to the Gentile world, here represented in the person of a Gentile (presumably a Roman) army-officer (or perhaps civil administrator)—'nobleman' is not a very good translation. There are two stories of the healing of Gentiles by Jesus in the Synoptic Gospels: the Syrophoenician's daughter (Mark. 7.24-30) and the Centurion's Servant (Matt. 8.5-13; Luke 7.1-10). It cannot be accidental that these happen to be the only cases in the Synoptists of healing at a distance; Jesus does not come into physical proximity with the sufferers. The truth is symbolized that, though Jesus never personally during his earthly ministry came into contact with Gentiles, the blessings of faith in him are intended for the Gentiles as well as for THE CHILDREN (Mark 7.27-29). It is hardly open to doubt that St. John's second 'sign', the Healing of the Nobleman's Son, is his version of the same tradition as that recorded in St Matthew's and St Luke's Healing of the Centurion's Servant. That event took place, as in St. John's account, at Capernaum. Moreover, St Matthew says that it was the centurion's *pais* who was healed—a word which can mean either ' servant ' or ' son '. Hence the Johannine ' nobleman's *son* '; St Luke, however, uses *doulos*, which properly means ' slave ' (see Matt. 8.6, RV marg.). The story symbolizes the pouring out of the blessings of Christ upon the Gentiles, as indeed St Matthew explicitly makes it do (Matt. 8.11). In St John's symbolism the living water has flowed out from Jerusalem, through Samaria, and it has now reached the Gentile world; as in the Apocalypse the river of water of life flowed from the new Jerusalem out of the throne of God and of the Lamb, refreshing the tree of life : AND THE LEAVES OF THE TREE WERE FOR THE HEALING OF THE NATIONS (Rev. 22.1 f.).

44. a prophet hath no honour in his own country
   This saying is recorded in some form in all four Gospels, but its context in the Synoptists is the rejection of Jesus in Galilee (St Luke specifies Nazareth, Luke 4.16; Mark 6.1-6; Matt. 13.54-58). St John at this point stands the Synoptic history on its head in the interest of his theological teaching. For him Jesus's OWN COUNTRY is not Galilee but Jerusalem; Jesus is the King of Israel, and David's throne was in Jerusalem. It was in Jerusalem that Jesus had been rejected : the Galileans received him gladly!—contrast Mark 6.1-6, etc. Jesus CAME UNTO HIS OWN [inheritance], AND HIS OWN [people] RECEIVED HIM NOT (John 1.11); David's city rejected David's Lord. For St. John Galilee is only on the periphery of the drama; it is theologically unimportant. It was what happened in Jerusalem that counted, as Jesus himself had taught (Luke 13.33). But St John is not deliberately contradicting the Synoptic history; his concern is with the meaning of events, with theological truth, not with biography.

45. The suggestion is that Galilean pilgrims at the passover festival in Jerusalem had seen miracles which Jesus had worked; but St John is not writing an historical account: he is not troubled by the fact that he has not yet related THE SECOND SIGN THAT JESUS DID (4.54). What St John knows very well was that the earliest Christian disciples were Galileans; that it was in Galilee that the faith of Jesus first struck roots. Even if Jerusalem was theologically important, the historical fact was that there were only a handful of Jerusalem disciples, and that the earthly mission of Christ in Jerusalem had (humanly speaking) failed. It was in fact those Galileans who had been with Jesus during Passion Week in Jerusalem who RECEIVED him and became his witnesses to the ends of the world.

46. a certain nobleman

The word *basilikos* means 'an officer in the service of the King' (see RV marg.), perhaps in this case in the service of Herod Antipas, who ruled Galilee and was popularly styled 'king'. The officer would, however, be a Roman army-officer, even if he were seconded to Herod's service.

53. himself believed, and his whole house

We are reminded of the accounts in the Book of Acts of the conversion of Gentile households (cf. Acts 16.15, 33; 18.8) and especially of the case of another officer of the Roman army, Cornelius (Acts 10.1 f.).

54. the second sign

St John has, as we have noted, assumed that there were other signs beside these two (cf. 2.23; 3.2; 4.45, 48). His meaning is that, amongst all the many miraculous deeds which Jesus performed, two signs bring out the real meaning of all that Jesus had accomplished; first the abolition of Judaism, now metamorphosed into the new wine of Christian faith; and, secondly, the fulfilment of Judaism (SALVATION IS FROM THE JEWS) in the pouring upon the Gentiles of the blessings of the Spirit of Christ.

V

THE LORD OF THE SABBATH

5.1-18

St John now treats a familiar Synoptic theme in his own characteristic way: the Son of Man is Lord even of the Sabbath (Mark 2.28). This meditation is reminiscent of and yet dissimilar from the contents of Mark 2. St John's third 'sign', the healing of the lame man by the pool at the sheep gate in Jerusalem, is strikingly like St Mark's story of the healing of the paralytic (Mark 2.1-12). In each case a lame man takes up his bed and walks, and a controversy with the Jewish religious leaders is provoked. But in the Marcan case the paralytic is brought to Jesus by four sponsors, whose faith is accepted by the Lord (2.5); in St John's story Jesus himself chooses the man who is healed out of a number of sufferers, thus illustrating an important Johannine insight (e.g. John 15.16, 19; I John 4.10, 19). In the Marcan story the controversy arises over the claim of Jesus to forgive sins, whereas in St John it is caused by the healed man's violation of the law of the Sabbath (carrying a bed is a form of work prohibited on the Sabbath; cf. v. 10). The controversy about the Sabbath occurs, however, in subsequent episodes of St Mark's narrative (2.23-28 and 3.1-6). Both St Mark's and St John's stories probably have reference to baptism in the early Church; man lies paralysed and helpless until the healing and strengthening power of Christ is received, with the forgiveness of sins. In St Mark's narrative the faith of the sponsors of the candidate is the vital matter; in St John's account it is the gracious, unconditioned invitation of the Lord which is emphasized, and the healed man's personal testimony (v. 15). Perhaps it was the analogy of the waters of baptism with the healing waters of the pool that led St John to transfer the setting of the healing of the lame man from its graphic Marcan context to its new situation in Jerusalem. But this must remain only conjectural; we do not know what other traditions St John was familiar with, besides St Mark. It is, however, entirely consistent with his method throughout the Gospel that he should thus make free use of Synoptic material and entirely refashion it for his own teaching purposes. Once again we notice that his aim is not simply to re-tell the Synoptic story but to bring out its underlying meaning.

2. in Hebrew Bethesda

Here and at 19.13, 17, 20; 20.16 we should doubtless understand 'Aramaic'; the expression occurs also in Rev. 9.11; 16.16 and not elsewhere in NT. The text here is somewhat dubious and 'Bethesda' may result from a confusion on the part of later copyists with the better known Galilean city; see RV margin. As the latter indicates, the second part of v. 3 and all of v. 4 are probably explanatory additions by a later scribe.

5. thirty and eight years

If this number has a symbolic meaning, we have no idea what it is. (The same is true of the FIVE PORCHES in v.2.) The three references in the OT to a period of thirty-eight years (Deut. 2.14; I Kings 16.29; II Kings 15.8) seem to have no relevance. St John is emphasizing that the man has been crippled for a very long time.

7. when the water is troubled

The explanation of the popular belief about the miraculous pool which is given by the scribe in v. 4 (RV marg.) doubtless states correctly the local superstition.

8. Arise, take up thy bed

The words are identical with those of Mark 2.9, which also uses the slang *krabattos* (bed, mattress, a soldier's camp mat), a word not much used in polite society. Its occurrence here supports the view that the Synoptic story of the Paralytic is in St John's mind.

17. My Father worketh . . . and I work

Behind this verse lies a thorough awareness of contemporary rabbinic discussion. The rabbis argued that the statement that on the Sabbath day God rested from his work (Gen. 2.2) could not mean that God suspended his continuing creative, providential ordering of the world, for otherwise the creation would pass out of existence. God must in some sense 'work' on the Sabbath. Jesus here asserts the same doctrine and adds that he too 'works' on the Sabbath. St John is thinking of Christ as the creative Word of God, by whom the world is upheld. The Jews rightly perceive that Jesus's reply makes him EQUAL WITH GOD (v. 18).

18. the Jews sought the more to kill him

St John here makes in his own way the same point that St Mark's Gospel has strongly emphasized, namely, that it was because of his attitude to the Sabbath that his opponents sought to kill Jesus (Mark 3.6). Whereas, however, St Mark particularizes these opponents (the Pharisees and the Herodians), St John, looking back upon the events from the standpoint of the Church which in his day stood over against Judaism, speaks continually of them as THE JEWS. This expression reflects the outlook of an age in which it had become clear that the Jewish nation as a whole (as distinct, that is to say, from individual Jews) had rejected Christ. St John brings out the truth (as the Synoptists had not done) that the very fact of Jesus's healings on the Sabbath in itself proves his divine nature, since it demonstrates his oneness with the eternal Creator whose providential activity can never cease. The doctrine that the work of the Son is one with that of the Father is expanded and developed in the next section. The healing of the lame man has become the 'sign' of who Jesus is— in his innermost relationship to the Father-Creator.

DOING THE WORKS OF THE FATHER

5.19-47

The unity of Christ with the Father is asserted as strongly as possible in St John's Gospel (explicitly at 10.30). This unity is manifested in their unity of action; the Son is active in all the works of the Father (5.19) and he does nothing which is not an expression of the Father's will (5.30; cf. 4.34; 6.38; 10.25, 32; 14.31). Thus, both the Father and the Son are jointly at work in the giving of life to the dead (5.21); the Son is appointed the agent of the Father's judgment (5.22); and the Son shares in the worship that is to be offered to the Father (5.23). It became a fixed principle of the Trinitarian theology of the ancient Church that the whole Godhead is active in the work of each Person of the Trinity: *omnia opera Trinitatis indivisa sunt.* This principle, already implicit in the NT, accounts for the way in which (for example) now Christ is said to be Judge (e.g. here and at Acts 10.42; 17.31; II Cor. 5.10, etc.), now God the Father is spoken of as Judge (e.g. Rom. 2.16; 3.6; Heb. 12.23, etc.); or again, Christ is said to be the life-giver (as here) or the Holy Spirit is declared to be the giver of life (Rom. 8.2; II Cor. 3.6): the Spirit is the Spirit of the Risen Christ, and the NT does not carefully distinguish between the two. The one God (who is addressed as 'thou') is active in all the operations of the Persons

of the Trinity (whom we may speak of individually as
'he').

21. the Son also quickeneth whom he will

The word for 'quicken' means literally 'make alive'.
The healing of the lame man, whom Jesus chose to cure, is
the dramatization of the principle here enunciated.

24. hath passed out of death into life

To have eternal life means in St John to be raised up at
the last day to the life of the redeemed in the age to come
(cf. John 6.40; see notes on 3.15 and 3.18 above). At his
baptism the Christian has passed through death into life;
he has passed out of the sphere of death into life, i.e., the
life of the age to come, which even now by faith (or
'eschatologically') he is already living.

25. The hour cometh, and now is

In these simple words the whole paradox of NT eschatology is expressed: Christ has come, sin and death are
defeated, the judgment has taken place, the Spirit has been
poured out in the latter days: we are already living in the
new age, which in one sense is yet to come and in another
sense has already come. THE HOUR means, of course, the
time of the consummation of God's purpose in history; see
note on 2.4 above, MINE HOUR. The ministry of the historical
Jesus was 'the beginning of the End', the opening act of
the final drama of history. This is the consistent point of
view of the whole NT.

the dead shall hear the voice of the Son of God

This is the truth to which dramatized expression will be
given in the story of the Raising of Lazarus (cf. esp. John
11.43).

27. because he is the Son of man

St John means, 'because he is the one who is foretold in

the prophecy of Dan. 7.13 f., where all authority, dominion and kingship are given to the ONE LIKE UNTO A SON OF MAN.' This Danielic prophecy, has, of course, greatly influenced the NT picture of Christ as Son of Man (e.g. Mark 14.62; Matt. 28.18; Rev. 1.7; 14.14, etc.). See also note on John 17.2 below.

28, 29. St John, in common with all the other NT writers, thinks that the judgment, which has now begun with the coming of Christ, will be consummated in a final day of judgment conceived along the lines of the later Jewish doctrine concerning a general resurrection, of which we find the earliest expression in Dan. 12.2. For St John, to possess ETERNAL LIFE means to be numbered already among those who shall rise at the last day to THE RESURRECTION OF LIFE, i.e. shall rise to the life of the age to come (cf. 6.40). It is in this sense that believers will not come into judgment, i.e. into condemnation. This would seem to be the NT point of view generally (cf. Matt. 25.31-46; Acts. 24.15; Rom. 2.5-10; II Cor. 5.10; Rev. 20.11-13). It is hard to deny that the NT teaches a judgment according to ' works ', but for St John ' good works ' means specifically to believe in Christ (6.28 f.).

32. another that beareth witness
St John returns once more to the theme of the attestation of the claims of Christ. The Baptist, a shining light amongst men, bears the highest human testimony to Christ, but there is a more than human witness to the truth of Christ's claim. God himself is the witness, first in the very miracles (' works ') which Christ performs in his name (v. 36), and secondly through the divine word in the Scriptures (vv. 39-46).

38. ye have not his word
Here God's word (*logos*) is his testimony; Christ is God's

final testimony to mankind, and he abides with his own (John 15.4-7).

39. ye think that in them ye have eternal life

The rabbis said that Torah was life in the age to come, and Torah was written in the Scriptures. It is in Christ, says St John, not in Torah, that there resides the life of the age to come, and the Scriptures themselves attest this truth. It was, of course, the firm conviction of the apostolic Church that the Scriptures of the OT testified in every part to the Christ who was to come (e.g. Luke 24.27, 44, 46; Acts 3.24; 13.27).

45. Moses was assumed to be the author of the Pentateuch by both Jews and Christians in the first century. The Torah in its more precise and narrower sense was identified with the Pentateuch; in its looser sense it was equated with 'the Scriptures' in their entirety. 'To set one's hope on Moses' means to believe in salvation through the Torah, to obtain by means of Torah access to the life of the age to come. But Moses himself (i.e. the Pentateuch) prophesied Christ; the first century Christians doubtless had in mind such passages as Gen. 3.15; 22.18; 49.10; Num. 24.17 and many others. St John means that the Pentateuch as a whole witnesses to Christ, but he himself provides evidence that he has in mind specifically Num. 21.9 (cf. John 3.14 f.) and Deut. 18.15 (cf. John 6.14). The unbelieving Jews profess to take their stand upon Moses, but in fact they reject his testimony.

VI

THE FEEDING OF THE MULTITUDE

6.1-14

The two miracles recorded in 6.1-21 constitute the only continuous passage in the Fourth Gospel, until we reach the passion story, in which St John seems to be following the Synoptic tradition without radically re-writing it. In that tradition a miraculous feeding by the Lakeside is followed by a journey across the Lake and the episode of the Walking on the Sea (Mark 6.30-52; Matt. 14.13-33; Luke, however, omits the latter miracle, 9.11-17). St John uses the story of the Feeding of the Five Thousand as a text on which to hang the profound meditation upon the Eucharist which follows in 6.26-65. In this, however, he is only making explicit what is already implicit in the Synoptic tradition. Already for St Mark the two Feedings which he records (the Five Thousand, 6.30-44, and the Four Thousand, 8.1-10) symbolize the giving of the Bread of Life first to the Jews and also to the Gentiles: the emphasis upon the *numbers* (cf. Mark 8.19-21) of the crowds, of the baskets taken up, and of the loaves and fishes, and upon the different localities, the different kinds of baskets, and so on, leaves us in no doubt in this matter. The Feedings were for St Mark Messianic signs fulfilling the Scriptures and pointing forward to the Eucharist in the Church and to the feast of the blessed at the banquet of the Messiah in the Kingdom of God (see Alan Richardson, *Miracle Stories of the Gospels*, London, 1941, pp. 94-9).

1. the other side of the sea of Galilee

The vague AFTER THESE THINGS does not, of course, adequately connect what follows with what has preceded. Until this verse Jesus has been in Jerusalem, not on either side of the SEA (or, in modern English, lake) of Galilee. St John is not interested in strict chronology or accurate topography. Here he is making a fresh beginning in his book of meditations on the life of Christ. It is as though he is now going to read a passage of Christian Scripture, or recite a section of the well-known tradition, which he will then expound in the sermon which he puts into the mouth of the Lord.

3. the mountain

Again topography is quite unimportant. 'The prophet like unto Moses' (see note on 1.21 above) is going to give the sign of the Bread from Heaven, as Moses had given the manna from the skies. THE MOUNTAIN is already a feature of the Synoptic symbolism: as Moses had given the former Law from a mountain (Sinai), so the new Moses gives his teaching on a mountain (cf. Mark 3.13; Matt. 5.1; 15.29; also John 6.15).

4. the passover

The point is important theologically rather than chronologically; the Eucharist is the Christian passover, and Christ is the Christian Passover Lamb (see note on 1.29 above), whose flesh is given for the life of the world in the living bread (of the Eucharist) (6.51).

7. Two hundred pennyworth of bread

This is the precise figure mentioned in Mark 6.37. The five loaves and two fishes of v. 9 also correspond exactly to the numbers given in the Marcan story of the Five Thousand; likewise also the twelve baskets of fragments in v. 13. These exact correspondences do not *prove* that St

John has read one or other of the Synoptic Gospels, but they suggest that he knew the Synoptic tradition very well and had observed the significance of the numbers (cf. Mark 8.19). Such details as the reference to grass (v. 10), however, seem to most scholars to be clear reminiscences of St Mark; the latter probably mentioned the GREEN GRASS (6.39) because he wished to fix the date of the incident at passover-time (grass remains green only for a short time in that climate). St John makes the point explicit.

9. There is a lad here

The introduction of the LAD (Greek, *paidarion*, ' boy ', ' servant '; cf. French, *garçon*) is peculiar to St John and is doubtless symbolical rather than historical. In the Church's Eucharist the ' elements ' (bread and wine) were taken from the gifts brought by the people; they were not supplied by the bishop (celebrant) or presbyters. The *paidarion* here represents the deacon who at the Eucharist of the Church presents ' the people's offering ' of bread and wine.

11. having given thanks

The Greek word is literally ' having made eucharist '. St John's representation of the fourfold eucharistic action (' he took ', ' he blessed ' or ' gave thanks ', ' he brake ', ' he gave ') is not quite so definite as St Mark's (Mark 6.41; 14.22), but his intention is clear. The Lakeside meal is a foreshadowing of the Church's Eucharist and of the feast of the redeemed in the Kingdom of God.

five barley loaves

The fact that the loaves were of barley is also peculiar to St John. He wishes to call attention to the fact that Elisha (Elijah's ' double ' in the OT story) had fed a company of hungry men with twenty *barley* loaves (i.e. small buns rather than ' loaves ' in our sense) (II Kings 4.42-4). Elijah was, of course, a 'new Moses', and Moses had fed the Israelites in the desert with bread from heaven (Ex. 16; Num. 11).

two fishes

The fishes are, of course, historical in the sense that the narrative is founded upon fact: Jesus fed the multitudes in the desert with bread and fish, however we account for the event. But probably the apostolic Church understood the fishes as the 'fulfilment' of Moses' other feeding miracle, namely the QUAILS FROM THE SEA (Num. 11.31). Quails, of course, are not fish; but then, manna is not bread. The parallel, however, remains: the new Moses, like the old, has fed the multitude in the wilderness with food from heaven and food from the sea.

14. This is of a truth the prophet

St John makes explicit what is already implicit in St Mark: Jesus is the 'prophet like unto Moses' (Deut. 18.15, 18; see note on 1.21 above).

THE WALKING ON THE SEA

6.15-21

In St John's narrative the multitude perceives the Messianic significance of the Feeding Miracle, for they wish to make Jesus king (v. 15), whereas in St Mark it is stressed that even the disciples had failed to penetrate his incognito (Mark 6.51 f.; 8.17-21). The story of the Walking on the Sea in both Gospels is concerned with the supreme mystery of the person of Jesus. The power of Jesus over the winds and waves demonstrates his unity with the God whose almighty power is frequently portrayed in the OT by the symbol of his control over the tumultuous floods and raging seas (e.g. Ps. 93). The mythology of the Creator-God who slew the dragon of chaos (THE DEEP) underlies this kind of biblical symbolism (cf. Gen. 1.2; Ps. 74.12-15). It was at THE SEA (i.e. the Red Sea) that the great act of new creation and salvation was performed by God at the Exodus from Egypt, after he had revealed his name to Moses (Ex. 3.14, I AM HATH SENT ME TO YOU; 15.1-21; cf. Ps. 77.14-20). All this symbolism would be in the minds of the earliest Christians who first told and heard the story of Christ's walking on the sea. St John hardly alters the traditional story at all. He does not append a long discourse to it as he does to most of his ' signs '; but we may tentatively suggest that his exposition of its meaning is postponed until 6.60-71 (see notes below), after he has first expounded the meaning of the ' sign ' of the loaves.

17. it was now dark

As elsewhere, darkness is symbolical (1.5; 3.2, 19; 13.30). At the date when St Mark told the story, it was indeed ' dark ', for the Neronian persecution was taking place: yet in the darkest hour the Risen Lord, no apparition, comes to his tempest-tossed Church, treading serenely on the waves of persecution and opposition, saying BE NOT AFRAID.

19. walking on the sea

It is true that the actual Greek words could be translated ' by the sea ', but it is unthinkable that St John intended such a meaning. In fact, he probably thought in terms of a *double* miracle—a sudden bringing to the land is suggested in the second half of v. 21 (cf. Ps. 107.30 and context).

20. It is I

The Greek runs literally, ' He says to them, I am; fear not.' The mysterious I AM (cf. Ex. 3.14) could not fail to impress itself on the minds of readers of the Greek Bible. Jesus reveals himself in his divine name (character) to those who have eyes to see. See note on 8.24 below.

THE EUCHARISTIC DISCOURSE

6.22-59

St John does not record the institution of the Eucharist, despite the length of his treatment of the occasion of the Last Supper (13.1–17.26). This is doubtless because the heart of the Christian 'mysteries' (sacraments) is not to be exposed to the uninitiated, into whose hands a written account might fall (cf. baptism; see note on 1.26 above). He conveys his teaching on the subject in characteristically allusive style in the form of a long discourse by the Lord on the theme of the Feeding of the Five Thousand. The contrast between the miracle as a merely physical happening and its deep, spiritual meaning is emphasized in vv. 26 f. It is possible to see the physical event and yet to fail to see what it signifies.

23. after the Lord had given thanks
These words are not found in some MSS and may well be an explanatory gloss inserted by an early copyist; this use of 'the Lord' is not the style of St John. But the expression 'where they ate the bread after the Lord had made eucharist' is conclusive evidence that the ancient Church understood the Feeding Miracle as in some sense a celebration of 'the Eucharist'. See note on 6.11 above.

26. not because ye saw signs
i.e., 'not because ye saw the inner meaning of the miracles.'

27. him the Father, even God, hath sealed

'To seal' in this sense is 'to attest' (cf. 3.33); God himself has attested the truth of Christ—doubtless in the descent of the Spirit upon him (1.32 f.). Baptism was regarded as a 'sealing' by the Spirit of God (e.g. Eph. 1.13; 4.30).

31. The story of the manna in the wilderness can be read in Ex. 16 and Num. 11, but the quotation in this verse is from Neh. 9.15, which calls the manna BREAD FROM HEAVEN. This identification of manna with bread makes the necessary transition to the bread of the Eucharist. The rabbis had come to believe that manna from heaven would be given again in the Messianic age (cf. Rev. 2.17), and St John believes that this expectation is fulfilled in every Eucharist in the Church, for the Eucharist is the anticipation in faith of the feast of the redeemed in the kingdom of heaven, at which the faithful feed upon the 'bread of heaven'.

35. I am the bread of life

i.e., life-giving bread. The life that is given is, of course, the life of the age to come, the life which is sacramentally or eschatologically begun here and now in faith. In vv. 39 f. it is clearly explained that this 'eternal life' means being raised up (from the dead) by Christ at the last day.

shall never thirst

The reference here is to the water which flowed from the rock in the desert when Moses struck it: WATER OUT OF THE ROCK is mentioned in Neh. 9.15, the verse which St John has just quoted. St Paul had already identified the rock in the desert with Christ (I Cor. 10.4); cf. also John 4.14; 7.37.

40. I will raise him up at the last day

In view of the solemn reiteration of this phrase in this chapter it is difficult to see why it should ever have been supposed that St John held Platonic notions about eternal life ('life outside time', etc.) or 'realized' eschatology. See note on 3.15 above.

42. the son of Joseph
Compare and contrast Matt. 13.55 and Mark 6.3.

51. the bread which I will give is my flesh
Here is made very clear the eucharistic reference. In the preceding verses it has been reiterated that Jesus is the true bread from heaven, the living bread, the bread of life (or life-giving bread), the bread of God, etc. Now it is explicitly stated that the life-giving bread is Christ's flesh: at the institution of the Eucharist in the Synoptic tradition (and in I Cor. 11.24) Jesus had declared that the broken loaf was his body. He meant that he was the Christian Passover-Lamb, and that the Supper was the Passover of the New Covenant, the memorial-offering of his one true all-sufficient sacrifice—what, in fact, St John has meant by the expression THE LAMB OF GOD (see note on 1.29).

53. Except ye eat the flesh of the Son of man
This verse asserts clearly that participation in the liturgical worship of the Christian community is the indispensable means of attaining the life of the world to come. The words EXCEPT YE EAT . . . AND DRINK . . . cannot refer to anything but participation in the Church's Eucharist.

54. The Eucharist is an eschatological sacrament; to partake of it is to share by faith even now in the life of the age to come and to receive the promise of resurrection at the LAST DAY, when God's purpose in history shall be consummated.

55. my blood is drink indeed
The introduction of the theme of blood into this context is the final proof that the reference is to the Eucharist: cf.

Mark 14.23 f.; HE TOOK A CUP . . . AND THEY ALL DRANK OF IT. AND HE SAID UNTO THEM, THIS IS MY BLOOD OF THE COVENANT . . .'

56. In this verse the aspect of the Eucharist as 'communion' is stressed; cf. I Cor. 10.16 f.

THOSE WILLING TO RECEIVE HIM

6.60-71

The theme of this section is the willingness of some and the unwillingness of others to receive Christ. The faith of THE TWELVE is contrasted with the unfaith of those who WALKED NO MORE WITH HIM. Apostasy is the ultimate sin in the persecuted Church of the later part of the first century (cf. I John 2.19, 23; apostasy is probably the SIN UNTO DEATH in I John 5.16 f.). The whole section may perhaps be regarded as a comment upon the story of the Walking on the Sea; cf. 6.21, THEY WERE WILLING TO RECEIVE HIM INTO THE BOAT—after his miraculous revelation of himself to them as the I AM who works the works of God over the rising sea and wind. Simon Peter's response to the question of Jesus and his declaration that he is THE HOLY ONE OF GOD (i.e. the Messiah) in vv. 68 f. may be regarded as the Johannine equivalent of Peter's Confession in Mark 8.29. (We may note that in the Marcan cycle of events Peter's Confession follows a Feeding Miracle, a a journey across the Lake and a discussion of the significance of the Miracle of the Loaves; Mark 8.1-21).

63. It is the spirit that quickeneth
i.e., 'that makes alive.' 'Spirit' should here be written with a capital letter. St John shares with St Paul the view

that the Holy Spirit, or Spirit of the Risen Christ, gives life (in the eschatological sense of that word which we have already noted); cf. II Cor. 3.6, 17 f.; I Cor. 15.45. The Holy Spirit is the earnest or assurance of our life in the age to come—not adherence to the letter of the Law. The Spirit gives life at our new birth (baptism); cf. John 3.5-8, where the contrast with 'flesh' is also found. (The different Johannine senses of 'flesh' may be studied in comparison with vv. 51, etc.) In John 7.39 the Spirit is identified with the living (i.e. life-giving) water.

the words that I have spoken are spirit, and are life

Again we should understand the Holy Spirit, identified with 'life'. The words spoken by the historical Jesus and recorded in the (Synoptic) tradition are vehicles of life when they are quickened by the life-giving Spirit in our hearts into living faith (cf. John 14.25 f.).

64. Again it is stressed that Jesus possesses supernatural knowledge of men's hearts and intentions and therefore of their future actions. See note on 1.47 (cf. vv. 70 f., and also 1.45; 2.25, etc.).

69. the Holy One of God

A messianic title, and one used in Mark 1.24 by the demon who with the supernatural insight of his kind (according to first century notions) penetrated the incognito of Jesus. St John doubtless alters the Synoptic THOU ART THE CHRIST (Messiah) (Mark 8.29; Matt. 16.16; Luke 9.20) in order to stress the fact that Jesus is of universal significance, not merely of Jewish-national importance; for some might think this was all that 'Messiah' implied.

70. one of you is a devil

The word used is *diabolos*, which elsewhere in NT is used of Satan ('the Devil')—e.g. John 8.44; 13.2. In 13.2

it is said that the devil incited Judas to betray Jesus; in Luke 22.3 we read that Satan entered into Judas. St John is saying the same thing here, but even more graphically. He is making the point (much emphasized in his Gospel) that the betrayal and crucifixion of Jesus were not unforeseen by him: Jesus had chosen the Twelve (not they him; cf. 15.16), including the devil-possessed Judas. What happened in the events of the betrayal and crucifixion had happened according to THE DETERMINATE COUNSEL AND FOREKNOW-LEDGE OF GOD (Acts 2.23): the Lamb was slain from the foundation of the world (Rev. 13.8; cf. I Peter 1.19 f.). The fact that Jesus was thus foreordained to be betrayed did not make the guilt of the betrayer any less heinous (Mark 14.21); *he* was not predetermined to make himself an instrument of Satan. In St Mark's account it is Peter who is called Satan by Jesus immediately after his confession of the Messiahship (Mark 8.33); St John perhaps wishes to emphasize the fact that, though Peter might temporarily have made himself the mouthpiece of Satan, the real instrument of Satan from this time onwards was not Peter but Judas.

VII

GALILEE OR JERUSALEM

7.1-52

The discussion of the true origin (*patris*, Mark 6.1, HIS OWN COUNTRY) of Jesus is carried on in terms of Galilee or Jerusalem. If it can be shewn that he 'belongs' to Galilee, then he is not the Holy One of God. Galilee may be historically important in the Gospel story, but Jerusalem is theologically important. Had Jesus died in Galilee, he could certainly not have been 'the prophet' (cf. Luke 13.33). Had his *provenance*, his spiritual home, been Galilee, he could not have been the Christ of God. It was from Jerusalem that the living waters would flow. These terms of reference for a discussion of Christology seem very strange to us, because we have learned to venerate (and with what compelling reason!) the Galilean story, the Galilean ministry, the Galilean accent. But for a Jew of the first century it was quite natural to carry on a debate whether Jesus was *the* Prophet (i.e. Messiah) in terms of whether he fulfils the scriptural prophecies about Jerusalem, the Holy City and City of David. It is relevant to notice that the Apocalypse makes much of the fulfilment of the Scriptures concerning Jerusalem (Rev. 21 and 22).

2. the feast of tabernacles

i.e., the Harvest Festival, the Feast of Ingathering in the autumn (Ex. 23. 14-16); it lasted a week, and on the eighth day (THE GREAT DAY, John 7.37) a solemn HOLY CONVOCATION was held. Along with Passover and Pentecost it formed the great triad of festivals of the Jewish calendar; it was the most popular of the three, and could be referred to simply as THE FEAST (cf. John 5.1, RV marg.). The devout built BOOTHS or TABERNACLES in the fields and lived in them in commemoration of Israel's sojourning in the Wilderness (Lev. 23.33-43; Deut. 16.13-15; Neh. 8.14-18). The use of water and lights was part of the ceremonial, to which oblique reference is made in John 7.38 and 8.12.

3. His brethren

Apart from 2.12 this is the only passage in which the brothers of Jesus appear in the Fourth Gospel. They do not believe that he is the Christ (v. 5), but they believe that he can work miracles, and they hope that he will shew them off to the crowds assembled in Jerusalem for THE FEAST. This is perhaps the Johannine version of Mark 3.31-34.

6. My time is not yet come

Jesus's TIME (*kairos*) is the same as his HOUR; see note 2.4 above. It is not yet the moment for the manifestation of his glory at Jerusalem, i.e. his crucifixion and resurrection. His brethren belong to the old order—to the time (YOUR TIME) when the Jewish festivals still have meaning.

10. then went he also up . . . in secret

One of the differences between St John and the Synoptists is that the former records visits of Jesus to Jerusalem before the last one. Here, however, St John is not entirely altering the Synoptic tradition; this is the final going up of Jesus to Jerusalem, which St Mark has also described as made in secrecy (9.30). But in the Marcan story, of course, it is for the Passover that Jesus goes up. St John brings out the point that Jesus went up secretly (though presumably with his disciples) in order to avoid the very publicity which his brothers wanted him to court. He stresses that there was much speculation about Jesus in Jerusalem (vv. 11 f.), as is very likely to have been the case.

15. How knoweth this man letters . . . ?

One of the unexplained problems of the Gospel story is how it came about that Jesus from the beginning was accorded the status and title of rabbi. At the start of St Mark's narrative he is occupying the place of the rabbi in the synagogue of Capernaum (Mark 1.21). St John's account here is probably his version of this Marcan scene: Jesus teaches with self-authenticating authority, NOT AS THE SCRIBES— not repeating the tradition he had learnt at the feet of a Gamaliel. He had NEVER LEARNED, i.e. had never been the pupil of one of the famous doctors. But whereas St Mark is content to note the fact that Jesus taught with authority, St John develops the point that his teaching is not his own concoction but is the teaching which God has sent him to impart. His authority is not that of some rabbinic doctor, nor that of the whole tradition of the elders, nor even that of Moses. He has no predecessors, for he is unique, the only one who can be described as A TEACHER COME FROM GOD (John 3.2).

17. If any man willeth to do his will, he shall know . . .

The whole biblical tradition stresses that obedience to God's will is the essential condition of man's knowledge of God. Knowledge comes not by 'thinking' or 'contemplation' (cf. the Greek *theoria*), but by *doing*—obeying, trusting, loving. 'The Jews' do not believe because they do not obey. Cf. John 2.9.

20. Thou hast a devil

St Mark records that Jesus was charged with being in league with Beelzebub; 'to have a devil' is a first-century dramatic way of saying that one has made oneself Satan's tool (Mark 3.22). John the Baptist had also been similarly accused (Matt. 11.18; Luke 7.33). Cf. John 8.48, 52; 10.20. See also note on 6.70.

21. I did one work

V. 23 makes it clear that the ONE WORK is the healing of the lame man at Bethesda pool in 5.1-9.

22. not of Moses . . . but of the fathers

Circumcision, of course, was instituted in the age of the patriarchs, often called THE FATHERS (Gen. 17.10-14). MOSES, i.e. the Pentateuch, commands it; see note on 5.45.

23.

Here St John again shews himself thoroughly conversant with rabbinic discussion and practice; to circumcise a child on the Sabbath, if he were then eight days old, was deemed to be meritorious as completing his perfection ('the better the day the better the deed') and was not an infringement of the law prohibiting work on the Sabbath. So, too, Jesus has restored a man to his proper wholeness or perfection on the Sabbath.

24. judge righteous judgment

Perhaps there is a reference here to the words of Moses in Deut. 1.16 f.; cf. 16.18 f.

27. no one knoweth whence he is

There was a belief, common in apocalyptic circles, that the Messiah already existed but would remain hidden until the appointed time of his revealing—whether he was the heavenly Man (Enoch 48.6; II (4) Esd. 13.51 f.) or an earthly figure, already living a human life somewhere in disguise. Jesus cannot be the Messiah because it is well known that he comes from Galilee (vv. 41, 52).

35. will he go unto the Dispersion?

THE DISPERSION (*Diaspora*, scattering) OF THE GREEKS (see RV marg.) is a technical phrase for the dispersion of the Jews amongst the Gentile populations (see RV marginal refs.). In characteristic fashion St John makes the hearers misunderstand the words of Jesus in order to emphasize their true meaning. WHERE I AM YE CANNOT COME refers, of course, to the abode of the ascended Lord and will be more fully explained in Chapter 14; cf. also 13.33, 36; 16.28 f. GREEKS, of course, means 'Gentiles'; on this whole theme see note on 4.43-54 above; also 12.20 f.

37. let him come unto me, and drink

The metaphor of the living water, already encountered in 4.14 (see note on 4.10 above), may have been suggested by the ceremonies of libation at the Feast. See note on 9.7 below.

38. out of his belly shall flow rivers

It is uncertain to which OT passage St John is alluding; RV marg. suggests Prov. 18.4. The meaning, however, is clear: the believer is a channel of life for others.

39. this spake he of the Spirit

The Spirit which was to be outpoured after the crucifixion and resurrection of Christ is the reality to which the metaphor of living water refers (cf. I Cor. 12.13: in our baptism WE WERE ALL MADE TO DRINK OF ONE SPIRIT).

for the Spirit was not yet

The RV translators rightly add GIVEN, for this is the sense of the passage. The outpouring of the Spirit upon all flesh, prophesied in the Scriptures, could not take place until after Jesus was GLORIFIED, i.e., in Johannine thought, crucified and exalted.

40. the prophet

The prophet 'like unto Moses', of course. See note on 1.21 above; cf. also 1.25, 45; 6.14.

41, 42. For the significance of Galilee and Bethlehem as

theological symbols see the introductory note to this section, 7.1-52. Bethlehem was, of course, the native town of David (I Sam. 16.1), and the Scripture had prophesied that the Messiah, the new David, should come from there (Micah 5.2; cf. Matt. 2.5 f.; Luke 2.4). St John must have known the tradition that Jesus was born in Bethlehem, one of the few points upon which the birth-narratives of St Matthew and St Luke agree; but, as is so often his manner, he is content with a mere allusion to the historical possibilities. For him the significant truth is not that Jesus came from Galilee or from Judea, but that he was come forth from God: the former truth might be determined by historical enquiry, the latter is known only through faith. Jesus of Nazareth (cf. 1.45 f.); Jesus of Bethlehem: both of these assertions are in their own ways true; but *the* truth is greater than any historical-geographical statement: Christ's true origin and home is in THE BOSOM OF THE FATHER (1.18).

48. THE RULERS are the members of the Sanhedrin, mostly Sadducees. Nicodemus, as we were told in 3.1, was a RULER; but if he was a believer, he was so secretly. When he cites Deut. 1.16 in favour of a fair hearing for Jesus, he is contemptuously charged with being himself a Galilean.

49. this multitude which knoweth not the law
We usually think of all the Jews of our Lord's day as being genuinely devout and regular in their attendance at the Temple and in the synagogues. Actually, of course, there were large numbers of the population who never went near either institution and made no attempt to observe the Pharisaic code of washings, food-laws, almsgiving, fasting, etc. They were denounced by the rabbis as 'sinners' (cf. the phrase PUBLICANS AND SINNERS). In the Synoptic narratives Jesus is upbraided by the Pharisees because he preaches to and eats with SINNERS (e.g. Mark 2.15-17; Luke 14.15-24). 'Not to know the Law' meant 'not to obey the

Law ' and so to be outside the People of God; this ' multitude ' of the godless figures in rabbinic writings as ' the people of the land ' (*'amme ha'arets*). Yet these were the very people who responded to the preaching of Jesus: THE COMMON PEOPLE HEARD HIM GLADLY (Mark. 12.37).

52. out of Galilee ariseth no prophet

If SEARCH here means SEARCH THE SCRIPTURES (cf. 5.39), it is doubtful what OT passage St John had in mind, and in any case a prophet had arisen in Galilee, namely Jonah; he came from Gath-hepher (II Kings 14.25) which was in Galilee (Josh. 19.13) (cf. RV marg.). Perhaps St John means to make the Pharisees assert that, if you search Galilee, you will not find any prophetic figures there, or that if you search the Scriptures, you will find that *the* Prophet (Messiah) will not arise in Galilee, since Bethlehem of Judea is the promised place of his arising.

THE ADULTERESS PERICOPE

7.53–8.11

Pericopē is a Greek word meaning a ' cutting ' or ' section ', and it is used by scholars for a passage, complete in itself, such as this one. This *pericopē* is no part of the original text of St John's Gospel and is not found in most of the oldest and best MSS. Its style and contents are more like those of St Luke than those of St John. It interrupts the continuity of 7.52 with the succeeding passage, 8.12 ff. It may have been inserted here by some copyist as an illustration of the word of Jesus in 7.24, JUDGE RIGHTEOUS JUDGMENT and of that of Nicodemus in 7.51. We cannot tell what was its original provenance or context in the tradition of the words and deeds of the Lord. These considerations, however, do not imply that it is not founded on fact. It might well have been preserved in the tradition as an illustration of the teaching of the Master, JUDGE NOT, THAT YE BE NOT JUDGED (Matt. 7.1). Apart from its setting in the Temple, it might have formed one of the group of 'conflict stories' in Mark 2.1–3.6; it described another of the attempts of the Pharisees to trap Jesus into a contradiction of the Law of Moses (v. 6; cf. Lev. 20.10; Deut. 22.22-24). The *pericopē* wonderfully illustrates the teaching of Jesus that no man is qualified by his own righteousness to condemn another (e.g. Matt. 7.3-5); judged by the standard of God's absolute holiness every man is an adulterer and worthy of death (Matt. 5.27 f.). Every man stands in need of the divine forgiveness which Jesus brings. He did not come to condemn the world but to save it (John 3.17); though we are all guilty before him, he says to each one of us, NEITHER DO I CONDEMN THEE: GO THY WAY; FROM HENCEFORTH SIN NO MORE.

VIII

THE WITNESS OF THE FATHER

8.12-59

How can we know that the claims of Christ are true? This is the question which St John is dealing with in this section. A divine claim requires divine attestation; no human testimony will suffice. It is God the Father himself who bears witness to the Sonship of Jesus. Those who do not know the Father, in spite of the claims they make concerning him, will not receive his witness, for they do not recognize that the words of Jesus are none other than the authentic testimony of God himself. Nevertheless the Father glorifies the Son (v. 54); the actual hour of his glorification is the 'lifting up of the Son of Man' (v. 28), that is, the crucifixion and resurrection. It is supremely in the crucifixion and resurrection of Christ that we know that he is the divine Son and that his witness is true.

12. I am the light of the world

The ceremonial of the lights at the Feast of Tabernacles (which is still the scene of this dialogue with the Pharisees) may have suggested this theme, as the libations probably had suggested that of the living water (7.38). The OT supplies plenty of material out of which the conception of Christ as the light could be formulated (e.g. Pss. 36.9; 119.105; Isa. 42.6; 49.6; Mal. 4.2), and the theme is well-developed in the Johannine literature (cf. John 1.4, 9; 9.5; 12.35 f., 46; I John 1.7; 2.8; Rev. 21.23; 22.5). It is not

Torah, as the rabbis claimed, that is light (cf. Prov. 6.23), but Christ. See notes on John 1.4 f., 9 above.

14. my witness is true

The true light can be measured by no other light than its own, for the reason that it is itself the ultimate standard of measurement. There is nothing else by which it can be evaluated. Therefore Christ's self-witness must be self-authenticating. He alone knows the truth about himself, his origin and destiny.

16. I am not alone

However, Christ's witness to Christ is not unsupported; the Father provides further testimony.

17. in your law it is written

The expression suggests that St John is reading back the controversy between Church and Synagogue, as it had developed towards the end of the first century, into the discussions of the historical Jesus with the Pharisees. The Jews objected that the claim of a crucified village teacher to be the Messiah was incredible, because it was based only on his own testimony and was not divinely attested; the Christians replied that the demands of the Torah itself had been met, that there should be two witnesses, by the fact of the double testimony of Christ and the Father. The law concerning evidence is stated in Num. 35.30; Deut. 17.6; 19.15. The Christians pointed to the resurrection of Christ from the dead (St John's 'glorification') as being the supreme act of divine attestation.

20. his hour was not yet come

See note on 2.4 above.

21. I go away

In St John this expression means that Jesus goes by way

of death and resurrection to the Father's abode, from whence he came. It is only by faith in him that we can be united to him in his death and resurrection and ascension. The supreme sin is to disbelieve in Christ; YE SHALL DIE IN YOUR SIN means 'in your unbelief'. Unbelievers cannot be joined to Christ in his death and resurrection, or, in Johannine language, cannot come whither he goes. For the definition of the root sin as unbelief see v. 24. Many Christians today find the assertion that unbelief is sin to be a hard saying; yet the whole Christian tradition down the ages has affirmed it. If unbelief is sin, faith is a virtue; but like every virtue we possess it is not something of which we can boast, for we did not create it for ourselves.

23. It has often been held that this kind of language about FROM ABOVE and FROM BENEATH (cf. John 3.3, RV marg.; 3.31; 17.14; 18.36; I John 4.5) is evidence of the Hellenistic outlook of the Fourth Evangelist. It is, in fact, the universal, archetypal imagery of religion in all times and places; it is as Semitic as it is Greek, and it could be paralleled in Norse saga or Japanese Buddhism; the men who built Stonehenge or the Aztecs of Mexico would have understood the symbolism quite well.

24. except ye believe that I am

The expression I AM (without a predicate) occurs at 6.20 (see note); 8.24, 28; 13.19, and 18.6. All of these passages bear a sense of the mystery of Christ's person. The I AM is at least a reverberation of the name of God in the Greek Bible (Ex. 3.14), as indeed it had been at Mark 6.50. The same Greek expression had doubtless carried something of the overtones of Ex. 3.14 when it occurred in other places in the LXX, e.g. Isa. 43.10. This verse (8.24) emphatically teaches that faith in Christ is the only means of salvation from sin and death.

26. See note on 17.8 below.

28. lifted up the Son of man

See note on 3.14 above. As the apostolic *kerugma* (proclamation) asserted, the resurrection of Christ was the divine authentication of his claims and teaching (e.g. Acts 2.36); it is the means by which we know that his revelation of God is true.

29. I do always the things that are pleasing to him

See note on 4.34 above and the introductory note to 5.19-47.

31. If ye abide in my word

This characteristically Johannine expression is more fully explicated in John 15.7 f., where the context illuminates its meaning; see also II John 9.

32. the truth shall make you free

Jesus himself is the truth (John 14.6; cf. 1.14, 17; I John 5.20), as indeed is implied by reading this verse in conjunction with v. 36. Mankind is in bondage until Christ sets men free; the thought of this passage is strikingly reminiscent of St Paul's teaching about slavery to sin and the Law (e.g. Rom. 6.20-22). The archaic word BONDSERVANT in vv. 34 f. should be translated 'slave'. The position of the slave, who has no permanent status in the household, is contrasted with that of the son of the family (v. 35; cf. Heb. 3.5 f.; Luke 15.31). Christ, who is Son in the Father's house, has conferred upon us the freedom of sons, which is contrasted with the bondage of the household slaves (cf. Rom. 8.2; II Cor. 3.17; Gal. 4.6 f.; 5.1). The metaphor is based upon the social organization of the ancient world, and it recurs in John 15.15, but it is not difficult for us to understand.

37. Abraham's seed

Elsewhere St John has shewn that Christ is the one to whom Moses testified; in this passage he claims that Abraham likewise points forward to Christ (v. 56). St Paul had already argued that the Gentile Christians, not the unbelieving Jews, were the true children of Abraham and the inheritors of the promise made to Abraham (Rom. 4; Gal. 3). St John, as the Baptist had done before him (Matt. 3.9; Luke 3.8), tells the Jews that it is a vain boast that they have Abraham for their father: Abraham's children would do Abraham's works (v. 39). But whereas the Jews seek to kill Christ, Abraham rejoiced at the prospect of Christ's coming (v. 56). To kill the Messiah is the work of Satan; those who work the works of the Devil are the sons of the Devil. If they had been the sons of God, they would have loved the Son of God (v. 42), but they cannot hear the word which Christ brings from God because they are eager only to do the Devil's work (vv. 43 f.).

41. We were not born of fornication

The implication of the emphatic Greek (WE WERE NOT BORN . . .) is that Jesus was so born. The earliest of such slanders as found in Jewish sources may date from AD 110 (so C. K. Barrett, p. 288). Here, as throughout this controversy, the Fourth Evangelist is reading back into the times of Jesus the debate between the Church and the Synagogue of his own day.

44. He was a murderer from the beginning

In the Johannine writings the power of evil appears as the diabolical caricature of the good. In this instance, just as Christ the truth was from the beginning (of creation) the life-giving Word, so the Devil was from the beginning (of creation) the murderous Serpent, who deprived mankind of immortal life (Gen. 3.4 f.; cf. Wisd. 2.24, BY THE ENVY OF THE DEVIL DEATH ENTERED INTO THE WORLD). The Devil

also is a liar: his first utterance in THE BEGINNING was his
lie to Eve (Gen. 3.4 f.). The Devil, as the caricature of Christ,
is the Untruth.

46. Which of you convicteth me of sin?

Jesus left behind him amongst his followers the indelible
memory of his own complete assurance of his sinlessness.
In any other person than Jesus the claim to be sinless would
be sufficient conviction of overweening pride. The Gospels
present to us the picture of one who, unlike all other men,
has no awareness of being sinful, and yet who was the most
sane, humble and selfless person who has ever lived. In the
biblical view, to *be* the truth is to *do* righteousness. Truth,
meekness and righteousness are the characteristics of the
divine majesty (Ps. 45.4).

48. thou art a Samaritan

The charge of being a Galilean (and therefore no prophet)
now gives place to one of being a Samaritan (and therefore
outside the Chosen Seed of Abraham). For the Samaritans
see note on 4.4 above.

and hast a devil

Perhaps Samaritan pseudo-prophets were regarded as
demon-possessed (cf. Simon Magus of Samaria, THAT
POWER OF GOD WHICH IS CALLED GREAT, Acts 8.9 f.). But
the charge is made in other passages in St John: 7.20 (see
note above); 10.20. In the latter passage demon-possession
seems to be quite simply equated with madness (cf. Mark
3.21 f.: HE IS BESIDE HIMSELF . . . HE HATH BEELZEBUB).

53.

Jesus is greater than Abraham: this is the truth which
the Church maintained against the Synagogue.

56. Abraham rejoiced to see my day

The Jews believed that God had revealed to Abraham

the mysteries of the future. St John reaffirms this belief and
claims that he REJOICED (cf. Gen. 17.17, LAUGHED—here
perhaps taken not as the laughter of mockery but of joy)
at the revelation of the DAY of the Messiah.

58. Before Abraham was, I am

Literally, 'before Abraham was born'. Christ was from
the beginning (of creation) the archetypal Word of God
(John 1.1-3). He was not only before Abraham but before
Adam. Note again the I AM without a predicate (see
notes on 6.20 and 8.24 above).

IX

THE MAN BORN BLIND

9.1-41

This chapter narrates the sixth of St John's seven 'signs' and the controversy which arises as a result of the miracle. In the Synoptic tradition the opening of the blind eyes had been set forth as the fulfilment of the Isaianic prophecies concerning the days of the Messiah (Isa. 35.5; cf. 32.3; Matt. 11.5; Luke 7.22). In particular St Mark had skilfully paralleled the theme of the opening of the blind eyes of the disciples (to the fact of Christ's Messiahship) with his miracle-story of the opening of the eyes of the Blind Man of Bethsaida (Mark 8.22-31). St John in this chapter likewise presents the physical miracle of opening the blind man's eyes as a kind of outward and visible sign of the opening of the eyes of faith. The spiritual blindness of the Pharisees is due to their sinfulness. Again the question is posed, as it has been in the previous chapters, Who is this Jesus? Only those who have had the gift of sight from the Lord himself can know the answer to this question. St John's teaching is fundamentally the same as St Mark's, but as elsewhere he makes explicit what St Mark leaves implicit (e.g. in the Feeding Miracles).

1. a man blind from his birth

The Synoptists have not narrated the healing of a man *born* blind. St John's motive is doubtless theological: mankind is born spiritually blind because of sin, and only Christ can enable man to see the truth, because only he can save from sin. YE MUST BE BORN AGAIN (3.7).

2. Rabbi, who did sin?

It was axiomatic in Jewish thinking that all suffering was divine punishment for sin—a very common superstition still today, as every clergyman knows. The criticism in the Book of Job of this simple-minded belief had not made much impression upon the popular mind. The disciples' question is therefore a natural one. Jesus, however, repudiates the implied suggestion; in Luke 13.1-5 he had rejected similar notions.

3. but that the works of God should be made manifest

It looks as if St John means that the man was born blind in order to give Jesus this opportunity of working THE WORKS OF GOD. But despite the Greek final construction (*hina*), the meaning is consecutive—' with the result that the works of God. . . .' The Semitic mind often expresses a result in the form of an intention (e.g. Ps. 51.4), but we need not be misled. In a similar fashion in John 11.4 it is implied that Lazarus is sick in order that God might be glorified. Of course, St John believes that everything that happens is the consequence of God's will, for what God did not will could not happen. But he is not a philosopher discussing abstractly the problem of free will; he is a deeply religious man who sees the presence of God in everything. He is aware, as the whole Bible is aware, that, although it is absurd to suppose that every illness or accident is an exact requital for sins committed, there is nevertheless a deep and mysterious connection between sin and suffering, as between sin and death. The power of Jesus to heal is therefore closely connected with his power to forgive sins (cf. Mark 2.1-12); the Greek verb ' to heal ', ' make whole ', is the same word as ' to save ' (*sozein*).

4. while it is day: the night cometh

The light of the end-time has appeared, and the true light is amongst men (see John 1.4, 5, 9 and 8.12 and the notes on these verses above; also I John 2.8). But the final reve-lation (the parousia) is not yet; Christ will GO AWAY; THE NIGHT COMETH. Until the parousia the true light is visible only to the eyes of faith. ' Night ' and ' darkness ' have deep symbolical significance in the Fourth Gospel; see 1.5; 3.2; 3.19; 13.30.

6. made clay of the spittle

St Mark twice records the use of spittle by Jesus in the working of a miracle (7.33; 8.23), the latter occasion being the healing of the Blind Man of Bethsaida, the ' paradigm ' of St Peter whose ' eyes ' were opened in the next *pericopē*. St Matthew and St Luke omit both references, perhaps because they were aware that pagan wonder-workers used such a medium and they thought the parallel unedifying. There seems to be no special symbolism in the use of spittle.

7. the pool of Siloam

From this pool in Jerusalem the ceremonial waters used at the Feast of Tabernacles were drawn (see note on 7.37 above). As St John explains, the Hebrew name is derived from the verb ' to send '. Jesus, as the evangelist reiterates, is the one SENT from God (cf. HIM THAT SENT ME in v. 4). The blind man is washed in the healing laver of God's Sent One; the forgiveness and healing flow from Christ, and the blind see. Shiloh is come (Gen. 49.10), and though the Jews reject the healing waters (cf. Isa. 8.6), the living fountain avails for the life of the world.

8. he that sat and begged

This touch may be a reminiscence of the story of Blind Bartimaeus (Mark 10.46).

14. In the controversy with the Pharisees that follows the miracle the legality of Jesus's healings on the Sabbath is re-introduced. See the introductory note on the passage 5.1-18 above—the Healing of the Paralytic at Bethesda Pool, a passage which has already dealt with some of the issues raised by the Healing of the Man Born Blind.

17. He is a prophet

The definite article is not used here, as it was at 6.14 and 7.40 (cf. 4.19). Yet the confession points in the direction of the Messiahship. Later Judaism sternly forbade the claim to be a prophet (Zech. 13.2-5) and regarded the age of prophecy as over—until the Messiah (THE PROPHET) came. See note on 1.21 above. If Jesus were a prophet, he must be *the* Prophet. That the Pharisees are aware of this implication is clear from v. 22.

22. put out of the synagogue

This verse is a clear instance of St John's reading back into the days of Jesus the situation of his own time. To confess Christ and to be excommunicated from the synagogue for this offence belong to the years of the expanding Church, when the rift between the Christian community and the Synagogue had become absolute, i.e. after AD 70.

25. one thing I know, that whereas I was blind, now I see

This classical description of the experience of conversion emphasizes the absolute distinction between the darkness and the light; those who have undergone it have no further need of proofs. Others, who have not experienced the saving power of Christ, may argue for ever about his divinity; those who have been brought to the truth by him know that he is FROM GOD (v. 33). *Christum cognoscere est beneficia ejus cognoscere,* and conversely those who have not experienced in themselves his redemptive power cannot be said to know him. Those who do not perceive that they need his saving

grace, like the Pharisees who trust in their own righteousness, will not come to know that Christ is the divine
Saviour, whereas contrite sinners who have been forgiven
and healed know it very well (cf. Mark 2.17). That is why
faith in Christ is a gift, an unmerited opening of blind eyes,
and why unbelief is sin. The real atheists are not those
troubled by honest doubt but those who trust in their own
righteousness. This is the heart of the evangelical theology
of the New Testament, and it is as central in the teaching
of St John (and indeed of the Synoptists) as it is in that of
St Paul.

31. if any man be a worshipper of God, and do his will

This is the consistent teaching of the prophetic faith of
the Bible, distinguishing it from all pagan religion. To
worship God and to do his will are synonymous: cultus
divorced from morality is an abomination in God's sight
(Isa. 1.10-17; Amos 5.21-24, etc.). The knowledge of God
comes by obedient faith (cf. 7.17).

34. Thou wast altogether born in sins

The Pharisees retort that the man is a sinner, as is proved
by the fact of his blindness. They, on the contrary, see;
they are not sinners and do not need to be preached at by
sinners. The self-satisfied, 'respectable' religious folk in
every age repudiate the contaminating association with
sinners which the preaching of the Gospel involves: LO,
THESE MANY YEARS DO I SERVE THEE . . . AND THOU NEVER
GAVEST ME A KID . . . BUT WHEN THIS THY SON CAME,
WHICH DEVOURED THY LIVING WITH HARLOTS. . . . (Luke
15.29 f.; cf. 14.23 f.; Mark 2.15-17, etc.). Had the Pharisees
known that they were blind, they could have been forgiven
and healed, but because they are confident that they can
' see ', their sins cannot be washed away (John 9.40 f.). Perhaps St John here is expounding the meaning of the sayings
of Jesus in the Synoptic tradition that the Pharisees are

blind leaders of the blind (Matt. 15.14=Luke 6.39; Matt. 23.16 f., 19, 26; cf. Rom. 2.19).

35. Dost thou believe on the Son of God?

Many good MSS read 'Son of Man' (RV marg.), but the difference is not in this context very important. Christ claims and receives the faith in him to which he is entitled from those who have experienced his benefits. This theological truth is read back into the historical situation of the Lord's incarnate life in a way which it is quite impossible to reconcile with the Synoptic tradition. But, as we have seen over and over again, St John is not writing history but meditating upon it. Cf. John 4.26 and the introductory note to 4.1-42 above.

39. For judgment came I into this world

There is a verbal contradiction here with John 3.17 (cf. also 5.45; 8.15; 12.47) but it is nothing more than that. It is everywhere implied that the inevitable result of Jesus's coming is judgment (e.g. 3.18-20), even though the primary object of the incarnation is the salvation of the world.

that they which see may become blind

St John has in mind Isa. 6.10, which (like St Mark at 4.12) he takes to be a prophecy concerning Christ which is now fulfilled. The inevitable result of preaching the Gospel of salvation is to harden the hearts and blind the eyes of those who trust in their own righteousness and imagine that they have no need of the physician. This is not the intention but it is the inevitable outcome of the preaching; and this is the meaning of the cryptic and difficult saying of the Lord in Mark 4.11 f., as indeed it was that of the original saying of Isaiah.

X

THE GOOD SHEPHERD

10.1-42

There are no parables in the Fourth Gospel, as we find them in the Synoptists, doubtless because St John is not (as they are) gathering up and editing the tradition of the words and deeds of Jesus, but is meditating upon that tradition as the Synoptists have recorded it. The allegory of the Shepherd and the sheep is the nearest that the Fourth Evangelist comes to presenting us with a parable; yet it is hardly a parable after the Synoptic pattern, because it does not really contain a story. The 'good' shepherd must be understood in contrast with the 'wicked shepherds' of prophetic denunciation. Before this chapter of St John is read, careful study should be made of Ezek. 34, in which the rulers of Israel are denounced because they fatten themselves but do not feed their sheep; God, however, will himself feed his sheep and cause them to lie down safely: AND I WILL SET UP ONE SHEPHERD OVER THEM, EVEN MY SERVANT DAVID; HE SHALL FEED THEM, AND HE SHALL BE THEIR SHEPHERD (v. 23). Amidst the political disappointments of Israel's history the hope came to be expressed that God himself would be Israel's Shepherd-Ruler and feed his flock in a green pasture (e.g. Ps. 23). St John in this chapter is contrasting Christ, the Good Shepherd, with the wicked rulers (the Romans and their puppets, the high priests, and of course the Herods) after the manner of Ezek. 34. But he never says that Jesus is the new David; nowhere does he make anything of the notion of a Davidic Messiah, except

129   E

perhaps in the question asked but not answered in 7.42.
This is doubtless because a Davidic Messiah would be a
merely Jewish saviour, a limitation which Jesus himself
refused (6.15); St John everywhere sets Jesus forth as the
Saviour of the world. We must, however, clearly understand that 'shepherd' in biblical phraseology means 'ruler',
and St John is claiming that Jesus is the ideal ruler of
prophetic expectation (e.g. Isa. 9.6 f.; 11.1-10; 40.11; Jer.
23.1-8; Ezek. 34.23 f.; Micha 5.2; Zech. 11.7, etc.). Christ
is the chief Shepherd of God's flock, the new Israel (Heb.
13.20; I Peter 2.25; 5.4), under whom the apostles and their
successors are under-shepherds ('pastors'), having their
allotted charges over that part of the household and flock
of God of which they are the overseers ('bishops') (John
21.15-17; Acts 20.28; I Peter 5.1-3). Perhaps St John has
taken the theme of his meditation upon the Good Shepherd
from the sayings and parables of Jesus concerning the
shepherd and the sheep as they had been handed down in
the Synoptic tradition (Matt. 18.12-14; Luke 15.3-7; Mark
6.34; 14.27).

1. the fold of the sheep
Lit., 'hall'; the courtyard of an eastern house into which
the sheep would be driven at night.

a thief and a robber
The allegory reflects the situation of the Church in St
John's day; there were many 'sheep-stealers' who preyed
upon the 'gathered' congregations in the great cities—
schismatics, heretics, false Messiahs, Hellenistic 'saviours',
etc. (I John 2.18 f.; 4.1; Matt. 24.5, 11, 24; Acts 20.29 f.;
II Cor. 11.13; I Tim. 4.1; II Peter 2.1-3).

6. This parable
The word used in the Greek is *paroimia*, not *parabolē*,
and it means 'a cryptic utterance', 'veiled speech'; it is

used also in John 16.25 and 29, where RV translates 'proverb' (but see margin). 'Proverb' is not a good translation in St John, though it is correct at II Peter 2.22, which is the only other occurrence of the word in the NT. St John never uses the Synoptic word *parabolē*, a 'similitude', 'parable'; the Synoptists never use *paroimia*.

7. I am the door of the sheep

The interpretation of the *paroimia* or allegory is now given. In allegory (unlike parable proper) more than one meaning may be attached to one symbol. Christ is the shepherd who enters in at the door (v. 2), but he is also the door itself. The meaning of this statement is explained very clearly in v. 9.

8. All that came before me are thieves and robbers

It is unthinkable that St John can intend Abraham, Moses and the prophets, or even John the Baptist, since all these testify to Christ. Perhaps he is not now referring to the 'sheep-stealers' of v. 1, the schismatics and false teachers who troubled the churches, but to the rulers who fattened themselves at the expense of the flock, the Sadducean high priests and Pharisaic doctors, the Herods and the Roman procurators. All these wicked shepherds (in the sense of Ezek. 34) had climbed into their places of domination over the flock by illegitimate means, and it was they who conspired against the divine Shepherd, who would lay down his life for the sheep and would gather together into one flock the scattered children of God (John 11.47-53).

but the sheep did not hear them

THE SHEEP will probably mean 'the true remnant of Israel', those who hear (obey) the calling of the divine Shepherd and who follow him, because they know his voice (vv. 3-5). It is implied in the *paroimia* that the Good Shepherd separates HIS OWN from the rest of the sheep (v. 4);

Christ leads forth the true remnant of the flock, the new Israel.

10. I came that they may have life

Christ came to save the true remnant of Israel and to give them the life of the age to come; see note on 3.15 above for the meaning of 'life' in St John. Christ's flock will have abundance [of life] in the age to come (RV marg.). Cf. 10.28, ETERNAL LIFE . . . NEVER PERISH.

11. I am the good shepherd

In the OT God has frequently been described as Israel's Shepherd (Ruler); e.g. Ps. 23.1. Moses also had been called shepherd (Isa. 63.11, RV marg, and LXX), but David was pre-eminently 'shepherd'. David had actually been a shepherd and had protected his sheep from lions and bears (I Sam. 17.34-37), as he had also saved his countrymen from Goliath and the Philistines. The idea of a shepherd risking his life for the sheep is a feature of the David saga; and the picture of David as the Shepherd-King enters into the traditions of Israel (e.g. Ps. 78. 70-72). He is remembered as the ideal Ruler and is contrasted with the wicked rulers who batten on the flock and leave it a prey to the marauders (THE HIRELING), and finally it is believed that a new David will arise to save and rule the flock of God (Ezek. 34.23 f.; II Sam. 7.16; Ps. 89.20-37, etc.). In this chapter St John is pointing to the fulfilment of Israel's hope, but since he believes that Jesus altogether transcends Jewish nationalistic aspirations he does not mention Davidic prophecies explicitly.

layeth down his life for the sheep

Israel's hireling rulers, the Sadducees and Herods, had fattened themselves while at the same time they had exposed their people to the rapacity of their enemies (the Romans). The Good Shepherd has exceeded even David's heroic defence of the flock; he has given his life for God's people (cf. 15.13).

16. And other sheep I have

St John now makes it quite clear that Jesus is no mere national deliverer but the Saviour of *the world*. He is not concerned only with Israel according to the flesh. The OTHER SHEEP are the Gentiles, amongst whom also there is a remnant who will hear (obey) the voice of the Shepherd. They shall become one flock with the remnant from the Jewish fold under the one divine Shepherd. Jesus did not found two churches, a Jewish and a Gentile, but one re-united new humanity (cf. Gal. 3.28; Eph. 2.11-22).

18. No one taketh it away from me

St John lays stress upon the fact that Christ's death (like his coming into the world) was entirely voluntary, an un-coerced act of divine grace (cf. 19.11; also Matt. 26.53). It was not the involuntary martyrdom of a helpless victim but a divinely willed act of salvation (John 3.16).

20. He hath a devil and is mad

See notes on 7.20; 8.48.

21. Can a devil open the eyes of the blind?

The Scriptures had affirmed that only God could do this; cf. Ex. 4.11; Ps. 146.8.

22. the feast of the dedication

That is, the anniversary of the re-dedication of the Temple in 165 BC after its defilement by Antiochus Epi-phanes (I Macc. 4.59). This took place in December and on account of its ceremonial was sometimes called 'the Feast of Lights'; for Jewish Christians it may have seemed appropriate from an early date that the coming of the Light into the world should have been celebrated about this time (Christmas). But St John makes no explicit reference in this section to THE LIGHT OF THE WORLD and suggests no symbolic significance for winter. It is pointless to try to fit the occasion into any precise chronology of the life of Jesus.

23. Solomon's porch

Again there seems to be no very obvious symbolism that we can detect. Nor can we precisely locate this part of the Temple. It appears to have been the regular meeting place of the earliest Christian (Acts 3.11; 5.12).

28. no one shall snatch them

St John is emphatic, as is St Paul (Rom. 8.38 f.), that nothing shall separate Christians from the love of God in Christ. God's love has laid hold of them and will not let them go; it is the strongest force in existence. Cf. also 6.37; 17.12.

30. I and the Father are one

On the unity of Christ with the Father see note on section 5.19-47 above. Because to be in Christ is to be in the Father, those who are in Christ are secure in the safe keeping of almighty love (cf. 17.11, 22 f.). St John's thought is Hebrew, not Greek; he is not making a metaphysical statement about the *being* of Christ and of God, though doubtless one is implied: he is asserting that the works which Christ performs are the expression of the will of God. It is a unity of activity which is primarily in mind.

31. The Jews took up stones to stone him

Stoning was the penalty for blasphemy (cf. v. 33) according to the Law (Lev. 24.16), but it could only be carried out after judicial trial and sentence. The Synoptists, however, record in different places that Jesus was accused of blasphemy (Mark 2.7) and that he stood in danger of mob

violence (Luke 4.29); it is therefore unreasonable to conclude, as some have done, that the Fourth Evangelist was
a stranger to the law and customs of Judea before AD 70.
He is compiling a meditation out of the Synoptic story, not
giving a new version of history. (It may be added that Acts
7.58 f. records a case of mob stoning such as is said to have
been impossible.) In the final trial of Jesus by the Jews he
is declared worthy of death as a blasphemer (Mark 14.64),
but since the execution is carried out by the Romans, he is
not stoned but crucified.

34. I said, Ye are gods
   This piece of rabbinic exegesis and argument is incomprehensible to those who have not carefully studied the
methods of the rabbis. It doubtless reflects the kind of
argument that took place between Jews and Jewish Christians. Briefly, Ps. 82.6 is quoted to shew that those to whom
the Law was given on Sinai (UNTO WHOM THE WORD OF
GOD CAME) had been spoken of by the irrefragable Scripture
as GODS in virtue of the divine gift that they had received:
how much more therefore was he whom the Father had
sanctified and sent entitled to be called SON OF GOD. (We
need hardly add that in the light of our critical knowledge
of the meaning of Ps. 82 such exegesis appears somewhat
wide of the mark.)

36. sanctified
   See note on 17.17 below.

37, 38. The miracles of Jesus are sufficient guarantee that
the Son is united with the Father in all his words and works;
even if the words of Jesus do not convince, his marvellous
acts should do so. Cf. 5.36 and 14.11.

40. he went away beyond Jordan
   Again there is no point in trying to make a connected

historical and geographical account, or in discussing
whether this section of the Gospel has been dislocated from
its original context. No rearrangements have proved convincing.

41. John indeed did no sign

Miracles were never attributed to the Baptist, yet his
testimony to Christ was wholly true. Had he been giving
testimony to himself, it would have been reasonable to
require of him supernatural signs as evidence. The Fourth
Evangelist has several times recurred to the testimony of
John the Baptist (1.6-8; 1.19-37; 3.23-30; 4.1; 5.33-36;
10.40 f.); this is the final mention of him in the Gospel.

the happening on the basis of faith. St John wishes us to understand through faith that Jesus Christ is THE RESUR- RECTION AND THE LIFE (11.25). The religious leaders of the Jews, he is telling us, understood this claim very well, and this was why they took counsel to put him to death (11.53). The truth of history which the Lazarus story contains is this: Jesus was crucified because he demonstrated by his mighty works that he was the expected Messiah. Had he been content to go about 'preaching' (in the attenuated modern ethical sense of that word), had he confined his activity to exhorting men to love one another and to turn the other cheek, had he even been content with denouncing the pedantic scrupulosities of the Pharisees and their pre- posterous 'tradition', the realistic rulers of the Sanhedrin would have left him alone; they knew well enough that 'preaching' is a harmless form of madness and does not unseat governments. They took action not because Jesus preached an ethic of love, as the old 'modernist' theo- logians supposed, but because he demonstrated the truth of his claim to be the expected Messiah by working miracles: if he had merely claimed by word to be THE RESURRECTION AND THE LIFE, they need have taken little notice, since Messianic pretenders must be taken seriously only when they are at the head of an armed rising. The chief priests and Pharisaic doctors agreed on this: the mighty acts of Jesus were such that, if they let him alone, all men would believe on him (11.47 f.). The meaning of the Lazarus story, then, is this: Jesus was crucified not because he preached the 'gospel' of love, but because he worked the works of the Messiah. The truth of history is that Jesus was put to death not as a good man, a righteous prophet, a religious genius or an ethical teacher, but as the Son of God. Thus, the 'truth' of the Lazarus story is far greater than a literalistic, unimaginative reading of it could reveal: it concerns not the resuscitation of one dead man, out of all the millions of human dead, but the appearance in the history of this world of him who is the creator of life itself, Jesus the Son of God, *the* resurrection and *the* life.

The reason for thinking that the Lazarus story is not literally true is not that it is difficult to believe. The Synoptic tradition records our Lord's own claim to have raised the dead (Matt. 11.5; Luke 7.22) as well as specific instances of this miracle (Mark 5.35-43; Luke 7.11-17), and the Johannine Lazarus story loses its point for us if we do not believe that Jesus could and did work such mighty works. The whole meaning of it lies in its insistence that Jesus was crucified because he worked the works of God. The difficulty about accepting it as literally true is that it cannot be reconciled with the Synoptic tradition. How could it be that the Synoptic Evangelists have omitted to record such a stupendous and public miracle, the deed which made the authorities determine to 'liquidate' Jesus? They, on the contrary, suggest that it was Jesus' action in cleansing the Temple which led the chief priests to their decision (Mark 11.18). It seems much more likely that St John is following his usual practice of meditating upon the meaning of the Synoptic tradition and giving us his interpretation of it in a form readily comprehensible in an age which loved to teach truth by means of stories rather than by abstract philosophical or doctrinal statements. Again, too, it is from the Synoptic tradition that St John has drawn his inspiration: St Luke had related a parable of Jesus in which it was declared that, even if someone returned from the dead, the unbelieving Jews would not repent (Luke 16.19-31). St John turns the saying into a story in which someone actually does return from the dead—and the Jews do not repent. Significantly the name of the person who has died is in each story Lazarus.

1. Lazarus of Bethany

Lazaros is the Greek form of the Hebrew proper name Eleazar (Aaron's son. Ex. 6.25, etc.), which means 'God helps'. Except in the genealogy of St Matthew (1.15) the name occurs in the NT elsewhere only in the Lucan parable of Dives and Lazarus. This Bethany is not the place of the same name mentioned in John 1.28 (see note above and RV marg.) and alluded to in 10.40, for that was in Peraea (beyond Jordan); this Bethany was a mile and a half from Jerusalem (cf. John 11.18) along the Jericho road by the Mount of Olives (Mark 11.1). Here Jesus repaired at night-fall after his entry into Jerusalem on Palm Sunday (Mark 11.11; cf. 11.19). Only St John says that Mary and Martha lived there, and he may have inferred this by reason of the doubtful identification of Mary with the Woman with the Precious Ointment of Mark 14.3. The sisters Martha and Mary are mentioned in the Synoptists only at Luke 10.38-42; they are met with in A CERTAIN VILLAGE—long before Jesus has reached Jericho. It looks as if St John has been bringing together various pieces of the Synoptic tradition and using them for his own purpose without much regard for biographical or geographical exactitude.

2. And it was that Mary which . . .

Here is fairly conclusive evidence that St John expected his readers to be familiar with the Synoptic tradition; he does not himself tell the story to which he alludes until 12.1-8. He has fused the story of St Luke's Sinner Woman (Luke 7.36-50) with the Marcan story of the Woman with the Precious Ointment (Mark 14.3-9)—whatever might have been the original relation of these two stories. In St Mark's story the woman at Bethany does not wipe Christ's feet with her hair, as is done in Luke 7.38; cf. John 12.3. It is, of course, conceivable that St John knew a tradition independent of both Mark and Luke, but in view of his reproduction of so many of their details (in 12.1-8), it is much more likely that he is following his usual procedure of adapting Synoptic material to his theological purpose: *entia non sunt multiplicanda praeter necessitatem.*

4. This sickness is not unto death

i.e., Lazarus is not going to die in the final sense; what is happening is a necessary stage in the glorifying of God by the death and resurrection of Christ (cf. 12.28; 13.31; 17.1).

9. Are there not twelve hours in the day?

Cf. 9.4; the DAY of the Lord will give place to darkness for a season before the parousia.

11. Lazarus is fallen asleep

The Christian conception of death as a sleep appears in Mark 5.39; I Thess. 4.14 ('those who sleep in Jesus'), 5.10. Cf. the word 'cemetery', from the Greek *koimētērion*, a sleeping-place, dormitory.

15. I am glad . . . that I was not there

The apparent callousness of this statement should not be taken too seriously in view of St John's absorption in the theological teaching of his parable; in any case Jesus's human feeling is stressed in vv. 35 f.

16. Thomas . . . called Didymus

St John translates the Hebrew 'Thomas' by the Greek 'Didymus', a twin (RV marg.). Thomas appears only in the lists of the Twelve in the Synoptics and in Acts 1.13. In the Fourth Gospel he figures more prominently (14.5; 20.24-29; 21.2). In this passage his touching fidelity suggests that his traditional soubriquet, 'Doubting Thomas' (based on 20.25), does him less than justice. Moreover, according to St John he is the first to confess the divinity of the Risen Christ. Early Christian traditions assert that he carried the Gospel to Parthia and to India, where he was martyred. Several apocryphal works were attributed to him.

17. in the tomb four days

St John emphasizes the *stupendous* character of the miracle: Lazarus has not just died, as had Jairus's daughter (Mark 5.35), but has been dead four days. Cf. v. 39.

19. many of the Jews had come

St John also stresses the *public* character of the miracle (cf. 11.42, 45; 12.9, 17); the mighty acts of the Lord were attested not only by the disciples but by many 'neutral' or even antagonistic witnesses.

24. in the resurrection at the last day

By the time of Christ the Pharisaic doctrine of a general resurrection had become the accepted popular doctrine. See note on 5.28 f. above.

25. I am the resurrection, and the life

Christ declares himself to be already that life-giving principle of resurrection which shall be manifest and active in the end-time; this is what his miracles have proved him to be. They are signs that the beginning of the End is already here. To believe in Christ is to obtain the life of the age to come.

27. thou art the Christ, the Son of God

See notes on 1.34, 41 above.

he that cometh into the world

HE THAT COMETH is a technical term in contemporary Jewish usage for the Messiah (e.g. Matt. 11.3 = Luke 7.18; cf. John 4.25; 6.14).

33. he groaned in the spirit

Here and in v. 38 GROANED means 'was angry' (see RV marg.). THE SPIRIT is not the Holy Spirit but means 'in himself', as in v. 38. Why is Jesus moved with indignation?

Not because the Jewish mourners are hypocritical in their sorrow, for no such suggestion is made; nor yet because they are sceptical about Jesus's power to work miracles: v. 37 implies that they believed that he could. A clue is suggested by Mark 1.43, where the same Greek word is used: Jesus is indignant that the leper's importunity forces him to disclose his Messianic power. St John means that the miracles of the Lord, though wrought because of sin (death) and on behalf of sinners, are yet the ground of his condemnation and the reason why his enemies are determined to slay him. It is in his miracles that Jesus is totally engaged in the assault upon the evil powers. By the miracle of the conquest of death sin is defeated at the cost of the Conqueror's own life. Cf. Heb. 5.7.

40. thou shouldest see the glory of God

For St John to SEE THE GLORY OF GOD means to know in our inmost being the glorious power of God's salvation. In this life God's glory is known to us through faith when we perceive his mighty acts of salvation. This is the truth that is being dramatized here.

43. he cried with a loud voice

Cf. John 5.25 (and note above), THE DEAD SHALL HEAR THE VOICE OF THE SON OF GOD; AND THEY THAT HEAR SHALL LIVE.

47. gathered a council

i.e., they held a meeting of the Sanhedrin; see note on 3.1 above.

this man doeth many signs

Here and in the following verse the clue to the meaning of the Lazarus story is found: the truth of history is that Jesus was crucified because he demonstrated by his mighty works that he was the Messiah. A Messianic claimant who could validate his claim was indeed a menace to the social and religious *status quo*, which the ruling classes found so congenial to their interests. The rulers (as the ruling classes in all ages succeed in doing) had, of course, entirely convinced themselves that their interests (OUR PLACE) were the true interests of the whole people (OUR NATION).

49. Caiaphas, being high priest that year

Caiaphas, son-in-law of Annas, had become high priest in AD 15 when Annas had been deposed by the Roman procurator. Devout Jews, who did not believe in the power of the secular authority to depose a high priest, doubtless continued to acknowledge the authority of Annas in some sense (cf. Luke 3.2; John 18.13; Acts 4.6), even though Caiaphas was titular high priest. Some have suggested that the expression BEING HIGH PRIEST THAT YEAR means that St John imagined the office to be vacated annually, and that therefore he could have had no first hand knowledge of Jerusalem before AD 70; but this is gratuitous. The words clearly mean: 'Caiaphas, who was high priest in the year when Jesus was crucified.' He was deposed along with Pontius Pilatus the procurator by the Roman Governor of Syria in AD 37.

51. he prophesied that Jesus should die for the nation

The Johannine irony is strikingly displayed in this passage. Despite Caiaphas's precaution—or rather because of it—the Romans did come and take away their place and nation in AD 70, and the words of the high priest proved prophetic in a sense which he neither intended nor understood.

52. and not for the nation only

Caiaphas's prophecy was more than fulfilled, for the scattered children of God include those beyond the limits of Jewish nationality. There were the OTHER SHEEP, NOT OF

THIS FOLD, whom the Good Shepherd MUST LEAD (10.16, RV marg.). The work of Christ was to gather into one the fragmented and warring sections of mankind, to build the Church, the new Temple of his body (2.21), to restore the lost unity of the human race, shattered by Adam's fall, in the new humanity of the Last Adam, the Son of Man from heaven.

54. a city called Ephraim

This small fortress town in the hill country north-east of Jerusalem is mentioned in the Bible only in some texts of II Chron. 13.19; there seems to be no symbolical significance in the reference.

55. the passover of the Jews

The presence of Jesus at the passover in Jerusalem is mentioned in 2.13-23; 5.1 (if the unnamed FEAST OF THE JEWS was the passover); 6.4; and again here. Those who hold that St John is writing a historical account have somehow to reconcile this lengthy ministry, extending over at least three and possibly four passovers, with the Synoptic history. We have seen reason to think, however, that St John's references to the passover are of a theological rather than a chronological kind and that he has no intention of re-writing the received tradition of the Church as it had come to be formulated in the Synoptic Gospels. See note on 2.13 above.

many went up . . . to purify themselves

To 'go up' to Jerusalem is virtually a technical term for 'make a pilgrimage' (cf. Ps. 122.4); pilgrims would arrive several days before the feast began in order to undergo the ritual purification which the Law demanded of those who would rightly observe the passover (Num. 9.10; cf. II Chron. 30.17 f.; John 18.28)

XII

THE ANOINTING AT BETHANY

12.1-11

We have already suggested (see notes on 11.1 f. above) that St John has compiled his story of the Anointing out of St Mark's story (Mark 14.3-9, followed by Matt. 26.6-13) and St Luke's (Luke 7.36-50), since he combines details from the two stories. We cannot here discuss the complicated question of the relationship of St Mark's and St Luke's narratives, in which there are striking points of difference as well as of resemblance. St John supplies some novel features of his own, such as the identification of the woman who performs the anointing with Mary of Bethany, and the attribution of the protest against the waste to Judas Iscariot. St Mark's motive had been to shew that the body of Jesus had in fact been duly and solemnly prepared for burial, despite the fact that the women who visited the tomb on the first day of the week had found themselves unable to carry out their mission of anointing the corpse (Mark 16.1-8). St John disregards this motive entirely, and indeed he departs so far from the Synoptic tradition as to describe the ritual anointing of the body of the Lord by Nicodemus at the burial (19.39 f.). In fact, he probably thinks of the anointing at Bethany not as a funeral rite, as in St Mark, but as a coronation rite: the word 'Messiah', 'Christ', means 'the anointed one', and at the Triumphal Entry into Jerusalem, which follows immediately, the city of Jerusalem turns out to welcome with hosannas the King of Israel (12.12-15). That is why in St John's narrative the Anointing *precedes* the Triumphal Entry instead of coming afterwards as it does in St Mark's.

1. six days before the passover

According to St John the passover began on a Friday evening and therefore Jesus's arrival at Bethany must have been on the Sabbath (Saturday) before that (i.e. the day before our 'Palm Sunday'). But since for the Jews a day began at six o'clock in the evening, the supper at Bethany would have taken place on what we would call a Friday evening.

Jesus . . . came to Bethany

The scene of the Marcan anointing was at Bethany, but it took place in the house of Simon who was nicknamed THE LEPER. St Luke's anointing takes place somewhere in Galilee in the house of a Pharisee called Simon.

2. Martha served

This detail is inspired by Luke 10.40.

3. ointment of spikenard, very precious

Compare St Mark: ALABASTER CRUSE OF OINTMENT OF SPIKENARD, VERY COSTLY.

anointed the feet of Jesus

In St Mark the woman anoints the head of Jesus; but in St Luke she anoints his feet and wipes them with the hair of her head. In St Luke, however, the woman wipes her *tears* from Jesus's feet, not the ointment (7.38), a point which St John has fumbled in making her wipe off the ointment. St John does not suggest that Mary is penitent, and indeed the mention of penitence is strangely absent from his Gospel.

the house was filled with the odour

The ancient Fathers took this detail (perhaps correctly) to symbolize the truth that the whole world was to be filled with the memorial of the woman's good deed (Mark 14.9).

4. Judas Iscariot

St Mark has merely said that there were some unspecified bystanders who objected to the waste of the ointment; St John makes Judas their mouthpiece, and furthermore adds some disparaging remarks about his character and conduct (v. 6). The Fourth Evangelist has come to believe that Judas had made himself Satan's instrument (see note on 6.70 above) and that therefore there was no limit to his wickedness. The objection to the WASTE is similar to one often made by self-righteous people in our day: is it not wrong to waste money on building a cathedral or buying a beautiful vestment, when so many poor people are not properly housed and so many heathen remain unevangelized . . . ?

5. sold for three hundred pence and given to the poor?

The words are a clear echo of Mark 14.5. It is hard to believe that St John can be following an independent tradition. Similarly the words of v. 8 are virtually an abridgment of Mark 14.7.

7. to keep it against the day of my burying

In St Mark the woman *breaks* the cruse; her action is not half-hearted or grudging: the vessel is broken and all its contents are poured out; the offering is total and irrevocable. In St John there is no vessel and no breaking; only a portion of the POUND of ointment is used; the remainder will be kept for use on the day of Jesus's burial. St John perhaps means that Mary was present with Nicodemus at the burial and anointing in the garden tomb (note the plural in 19.40—though it may refer to Joseph of Arimathea and Nicodemus only).

THE TRIUMPHAL ENTRY

12.12-19

Whereas the Synoptic accounts represent the 'triumph' given to Jesus on his entry into Jerusalem as having been staged mainly by his own entourage (see esp. Luke 19.37), St John represents it as a remarkable public ovation: a great multitude went out to meet him and acclaimed him as the Messiah, to the chagrin of the Pharisees. According to St Mark the secret that Jesus is the Messiah has leaked out, despite his commands to silence; a blind beggar has hailed him as David's Son (i.e. Messiah; Mark 10.47 f.). Jesus therefore enacts a brilliant piece of teaching, in circumstances in which reasoned instruction would have been impossible, to demonstrate what kind of a Messiah he is. He rides into Jerusalem not on a war-horse but on an ass, thus dramatizing the prophecy of Zech. 9.9, REJOICE . . . O DAUGHTER OF JERUSALEM: BEHOLD, THY KING COMETH UNTO THEE: HE IS JUST, AND HAVING SALVATION; LOWLY, AND RIDING UPON AN ASS. . . . At the same time Jesus publicly claims that he is Zion's (Messianic) King and renounces the Zealots' conception of a military national hero-Messiah. David's Son comes to receive his inheritance of David's city and throne, but he is acclaimed not, as in the triumph of a conquering Caesar, by the plaudits of his men of war but by the hosannas of his peasant followers; his victorious banners are palm branches hastily cut from the trees by the roadside (Mark 11.7-10; cf. Matt. 21.4-11; Luke 19.35-40). St John seems to have no other source than this material of the Synoptic tradition. For him also the trium-

phal scene dramatizes the coming of the expected Davidic
King to claim 'his own', but for the reasons already dis-
cussed (see the introductory note to 10.1-42 and notes on
10.11, 14 above) he does not make explicit (as Mark has
done) the Davidic theme (Mark 11.10). In St John Jesus is
hailed as King of Israel, the very charge on which he was
subsequently tried and executed (18.33-40; 19.1-3, 12, 19):
he has already been symbolically anointed King—by a
woman; he will wear a royal robe of purple and a
monarch's crown—of thorns; he will be lifted up and en-
throned—upon a cross. This is his 'glorification', of which
the triumphal entry is a prelude and sign (12.16); and in
spite of all their scheming the Pharisees will prevail
nothing; the whole world will go after him (12.19).

13. Hosanna: Blessed is he that cometh

The words (as in Mark 11.9) are cited from Ps. 118.25 f.;
SAVE NOW, WE BESEECH THEE, O YAHWEH . . . BLESSED IN
THE NAME OF YAHWEH IS HE THAT COMETH. (Note that the
sense is 'blessed in the name of the Lord', not 'that cometh
in the name of the Lord'.) By NT times 'he that cometh'
had become a technical term for the Messiah (see note on
11.27 above). 'Hosanna' is a Hebrew word, retained in the
Greek of Mark 10.11, etc., meaning 'Save (us), we beseech
(thee)'; it was chanted liturgically in procession and thus
had doubtless passed untranslated into the vocabulary of
the Greek-speaking Christian churches; cf. *Maran atha*
(I Cor. 16.22).

16. These things understood not his disciples at the first

It is a characteristic theme of St John's that the disciples
did not understand the real meaning of the words and
deeds of Jesus until after his 'glorification' and the coming
of the Holy Spirit (13.7; 14.26; 16.12 f.). This doubtless
represents the historical situation, but it is not a principle
which St John chooses to observe in the manner in which

he tells his Gospel story: he shews us the disciples as knowing all about who Jesus is from the first moment of their
encounter with him (1.41, etc.), in strong contrast with St
Mark. As a matter of fact, the principle fits the episode of
the Triumphal Entry rather badly: at least here—as in St
Mark—the disciples must have had a fair inkling of what
was being proclaimed when they took their part in the
dramatization of Zechariah's prophecy concerning Zion's
King.

'THE HOUR IS COME'

12.20-50

The HOUR has now come for the Son of Man to be GLORI-
FIED (v. 23). It is precipitated by the demand of the GREEKS
—the whole wide world—for the revelation of Jesus (v. 21).
It is by his glorification, i.e., crucifixion and resurrection,
that the revelation is to be made to the world. Salvation is
from the Jews (4.22), and the King of Israel, now duly
acclaimed in Jerusalem, will be made known as the true
Light and Saviour of the world. This section sums up the
self-disclosure which Jesus has made to 'the Jews', and
many of the themes which have been dealt with in the preceding sections are mentioned again. The divine voice from
heaven proclaims the glorification of the Father's name in
the lifting up of the Son of Man, by which all men are to be
drawn into the unity of the Father and the Son (vv. 29-32).
The section thus provides a bridge to the story of the glorification (the passion story and its corollary, the gospel of
the resurrection and ascension of Christ), to which all that
has gone before has pointed. The rejection of Christ by
his own people, foretold by Isaiah (vv. 38-41), is the dark
background against which there shines more brightly the

Light which is come not for judgment but for the salvation of the world (vv. 46 f.).

20. Greeks

The word does not, of course, mean natives of Greece but simply ' non-Jews ' (as, clearly, in Mark 7.26; cf. John 7.35).

went up to worship

For the expression WENT UP see note on 11.55 above. The GREEKS whom St John has in mind would be ' God-fearers ', i.e. devout non-Jews who were attracted by the monotheism and high moral seriousness of Judaism, and who attended synagogue worship and sometimes came as pilgrims to the Temple in Jerusalem (cf. Acts 17.4, 17).

23. The hour is come

St John does not record whether the GREEKS saw Jesus; the implication is that they did not. The blessings of the Messiah could not be communicated to the Gentile world until after his death and exaltation. Their presence is symbolic; they represent the whole world, which is eagerly awaiting THE DESIRE OF ALL NATIONS (Hag. 2.7). When Jesus hears of their arrival, he declares that his HOUR IS COME, the long awaited ' glorification ' by which through death and resurrection he ascends to the Father, resuming the glory which he had with the Father BEFORE THE WORLD WAS (John 17.5). For the Johannine sense of ' hour ' see note on 2.4 above.

24. Except a grain of wheat

Jesus in the Synoptic tradition had frequently drawn parables from the germination of seeds (Mark 4.2-9, 26-32, etc.).

25. He that loveth his life

St John's version of the familiar Synoptic material (Matt. 10.39; Mark 8.34 f.; Luke 9.23 f.; 17.33).

27. Father, save me from this hour

This is the Johannine equivalent of the Synoptic account of the Agony in Gethsemane. In Mark 14.35 Jesus prays that THE HOUR MIGHT PASS AWAY FROM HIM; in 14.41 he declares THE HOUR IS COME. Nevertheless the contrast with the Marcan account is very noticeable: in St John there is no weakness, no doubting; and the Father's voice from heaven proclaims the fulfilment of the divine plan. St John makes it clear that Jesus himself needed no reassuring by a heavenly voice: THIS VOICE CAME NOT FOR MY SAKE, BUT FOR YOUR SAKES (v. 30; cf. 11.42).

28. a voice out of heaven

In the Synoptic records the voice from heaven is heard at the Baptism and Transfiguration of Jesus (Mark 1.11; 9.7 and parallels), neither of which events is recorded in the Fourth Gospel. St John emphasizes the dread solemnity of this moment (the arrival of the hour of glorification) by the same device of the heavenly voice. The latter is frequently met with in rabbinic narratives and is known as *bath qol* (lit. ' daughter of the voice ', i.e., the *echo* of God's voice); this is identified with thunder (cf. v. 29), which was regarded as an *echo* of God's voice, and which was held on occasion to utter intelligible words. In all four Gospels, however, it is no mere echo of God's voice that is heard, but the direct speaking of the Father to the Son.

I have both glorified it

This probably means that the true glory of Jesus has been manifested in the ' signs '; cf. 2.11; 9.3; 11.4, 40. The Synoptists have set forth the Transfiguration of Christ as a glorification—St Matthew and St Mark implicitly, St Luke explicitly (Luke 9.31); if St John is thinking of this episode as a parallel to the Synoptists' Transfiguration story, he will also mean that God has glorified Jesus by speaking to him out of heaven.

and will glorify it again
i.e., in the events of the passion and exaltation of Christ
(17.1, 5) and in his Church (17.10).

31. Now is the judgment of this world
In the Johannine presentation that which is outward and
visible is the precise opposite of what is *really* true: Pilate
appears to judge Jesus, but it is really Jesus who judges
Pilate and through him all the secular powers of this world.

now shall the prince of this world be cast out
But the secular powers, when they pervert their God-
appointed ministry (cf. Rom. 13.1-7), are themselves only
the agents and tools of Satan, the prince of this world, who
has usurped the place of God and subjected the world to
his evil reign (cf. I John 5.19). Christ's judgment of Satan
has now begun; the house of the Strong Man is being invaded and despoiled by a stronger deliverer, and his kingdom is at an end (Mark 3.27). The victorious cross is the
instrument by which Satan is conquered and his prisoners
set free (cf. Col. 2.14 f.). Pilate's Judgment Hall is the locus
in time and space of the cosmic judgment that is accomplished by Christ the Conqueror.

32. See notes on 3.14 and 8.28 above.

34. The Christ abideth for ever
The phrase THE LAW in its wider sense could mean 'the
Scriptures', not only the Pentateuch. The references are
probably to Pss. 89.4; 110.4; Isa. 9.7; Ezek. 37.25; Dan.
2.44; 7.14, 18, 27; cf. Luke 1.33; Heb. 1.8; Rev. 11.15.

35, 36. Cf. John 1.9; 8.12; 9.4 f.; 12.46.

38. the word of Isaiah the prophet
To the NT writers there was, of course, only one Isaiah.

They held that he had predicted the unbelief of the Jews and their rejection of the Messiah; cf. Mark 4.12 (citing Isa. 6.10, which is cited by St John in v. 40); Rom. 10.16 (citing Isa. 53.1, cited by St John in v. 38). St John says that the glory of the Lord which Isaiah saw in the Temple (Isa. 6.1) was the glory of the pre-existent Christ (cf. John 5.39; 8.56-8).

43. they loved the glory of men

The Greek word *doxa* in everyday usage could mean nothing more than 'good opinion', 'repute', and it is only in its developed biblical-theological use that it carries the full content which is usually found in St John's employment of it (see note on 1.14 above, WE BEHELD HIS GLORY). Here St John plays on the double sense of the word.

44-50.

These verses echo a number of themes which have already been developed by the Evangelist in previous chapters. (See RV marginal notes for references and the notes upon these passages above.) The abiding word or message which Christ has spoken from the Father will be the standard of judgment by which all shall be judged on the last day; but those who believe and obey the words of Christ shall not be judged (condemned) but shall have the life of the age to come which lies beyond the final judgment. Thus St John summarizes and concludes his account of the *public* ministry of Jesus. He now begins the story of the passion and the resurrection, and henceforward the teaching which Jesus gives is addressed to his band of chosen disciples. For v. 49 see note on 17.8 below.

XIII

THE FOOT-WASHING AT THE SUPPER

13.1-20

It is characteristic of St John's method that he should preface the teaching which Jesus gives to his disciples at their last supper together with an enacted parable. It stands to the discourse that follows in very much the same relation as certain of the 'signs' have stood to the teaching which has followed and expounded them (e.g. Chapters 5, 6 or 9). Indeed the action of Jesus in washing the disciples' feet is a sign, though it is not a miraculous one and therefore is not spoken of by St John as a sign; it is an action which bears profound significance, like the Cleansing of the Temple or the Triumphal Entry into Jerusalem. It foreshadows the cross itself: the voluntary humility of the Lord cleanses his loved ones and gives to them an example of selfless service which they must follow.

1. Now before the feast of the passover
Here we encounter a notable point of contradiction between St John and the Synoptic accounts. For the Synoptists the Last Supper of Jesus with his disciples on the night on which he was betrayed was a passover meal: for St John it takes place on the *eve* of the passover (cf. also 18.28; 19.14, 31, 42) and could not therefore have been the passover meal. The question which of the two assertions is right is exceedingly complicated, and a vast literature has been written about it (see J. Jeremias, *The Eucharistic Words of Jesus,* Eng. trans. 1955; A. J. B. Higgins, *The Lord's Supper*

in the NT, 1952). Here we would make only three observations. First, we have so often noticed the freedom with which St John treats the Synoptic history in order to serve his theological purposes that we shall hardly be surprised to find him once more taking liberties with the received tradition, especially if we discover that he has a very good didactic object in view (see note on 19.14 below). Secondly, no very serious theological issues are raised by the question whether the Last Supper was or was not a passover meal; it occurred at passover-time, and the interpretation of Christ's death remains valid (cf. I Cor. 5.7), as indeed it does for St John (see notes on 1.29 above and 19.14 below). Thirdly, the omission by St John of the words of Jesus at the breaking of the bread and at the giving of the cup is significant in this regard. It is due (as suggested in the note on 1.26 above) to his desire to withhold the sacramental mysteries from inspection by pagan eyes, not to any failure to appreciate the Church's sacramental doctrine and worship (see notes on 6.51, 53 and 55 above); but it makes easier the omission of any reference to the supper as a passover meal. St John well knew that the Lord's words implied that the eucharistic loaf and cup constituted the Christian paschal offerings, since Christ himself was the Christian paschal lamb. But he prefers to develop this truth in a quite different way (see on 19.14 below).

his hour was come that he should depart . . .

Cf. 12.33 (and note above). St John is deeply aware of the significance of the fact that the hour of Christ's glorification was the time of the passover commemoration of the exodus-redemption of Israel and of the eschatological anticipation of the greater redemption which it foreshadowed, when God would make a new covenant with the house of Israel.

2. See note on 6.70 above; cf. also 12.4-6.

4. layeth aside his garments . . . took a towel

The actions are symbolical. Jesus lays down his garments —assuming the dress and posture of a slave—in order to serve his disciples and make them clean: so he will lay down his robe of flesh and die to save and cleanse his Church. St John is dramatizing the teaching preserved in the Synoptic tradition that THE SON OF MAN CAME NOT TO BE MINISTERED UNTO BUT TO MINISTER (Mark 10.45, etc.); perhaps he has specially in mind the sayings recorded in St Luke's Gospel in the context of the Last Supper, especially 22.27. I AM IN THE MIDST OF YOU AS HE THAT SERVETH. Thus, once again, while St John has added a new theme, he has simply brought out the Synoptic teaching in his own parabolic manner.

12. sat down again

Literally ' reclined ' (see RV marg.)—in oriental fashion. Our mental picture of the Last Supper, with the company sitting up at table as if having their portrait taken, is of course derived from mediaeval and renaissance art, which unashamedly portrayed Gospel scenes against a contemporary background.

13. Master, and Lord

The disciples addressed Jesus as *Rabbi* and *Mari* (Gk. *Kurios*); for ' rabbi ' see note on 1.38 above. LORD could be nothing more than a title of respect, as in 4.11 (see RV marg.), but in view of its later Christian usage it is probable that St John thinks of it as implying divine honours. It would be the duty of the youngest member of the group of disciples attached to a rabbi to perform such acts of menial service as foot-washing.

16. a servant is not greater than his lord

The Greek nouns are *doulos*, lit. ' slave ', and *kurios*. One meaning of *kurios* is ' slave-owner '; cf. Eph. 6.5, 9

(with RV marg.); Col. 3.22, etc.; John 15.15. The Synoptic
version of the saying is found in Matt. 10.24; see also v.
20 below.

one that is sent

The Greek is literally 'an apostle', St John's only use
of the noun. Though it is not here used technically, its
technical use could hardly have been absent from St John's
mind, and we would probably be right in thinking that he
is implying that the bishops and presbyters of the Church
must not lord it over the flock (cf. I Peter 5.3; III John 9.)

17. Cf. Luke 11.28.

18, 19. St John is insistent that nothing took Jesus by surprise or happened against his intention (cf. 2.24 f.; 19.11,
etc.). The quotation is from Ps. 41.9, which the early Church
naturally took to be a prophecy of Judas's betrayal.

19. The fact that Jesus predicted everything that should
happen, including Judas's betrayal and Peter's denial—like
the fact that the whole story was foretold even in its details
by the Scriptures—is manifest proof of the divine authen-
ticity of the Gospel. On the I AM see note on 8.24 above.

20. The Synoptic versions of this saying will be found at
Matt. 10.40; 18.5; Luke 10.16; Mark 9.37. Cf. also Gal 4.14;
John 12.44 f.; Matt. 25.40.

JUDAS AND PETER

13.21-38

In this section St John illustrates his assertion in v. 19

above, that Jesus could predict what was going to happen
with complete divine foreknowledge. He uses for this purpose two themes from the traditional story of the passion,
the betrayal by Judas and the denial by Peter. The Synoptic
Gospels had already related Jesus's predictions of both
events during the Supper (Mark 14.18-21, 29-31 and
parallels); St John is not adding new material but bringing
out the significance of the old. His introduction of the
Beloved Disciple (v. 23) is, of course, entirely new, as this
figure is unknown to the Synoptists; it raises acute historical
questions, and the problem of his identity—and indeed of
his existence—remains unsolved. Certainly St John here
raises a difficulty that is absent from St Mark and St Luke,
in whose accounts the betrayer is not named by Jesus and
there is no departure of Judas during the supper (but contrast Matt. 26.25); if Jesus had specified that the betrayer
was Judas, why did not the other disciples stop him? St
John himself clearly noticed the difficulty (vv. 28 f.), but
his attempt to explain it away is not entirely convincing.
Again we must note that St John's dramatic scenes are
theological parables rather that historical reminiscence or
biographical reportage.

21. he was troubled in the spirit

As at 11.33 it is Jesus's human spirit, not the Holy Spirit,
that is intended; cf. 12.27.

23. reclining in Jesus' bosom

During the meal the diner reclined on his left side, with
the right arm free for use; the person on the right of the
host had his head close to his breast and could speak in-
timately with him. The expression IN HIS BOSOM is thus an
idiom for ' at his side '—' in closest proximity with '--and
does not imply physical contact. St John wishes to suggest
that a deep spiritual *rapport* existed between Christ and
the Beloved Disciple (cf. the expression ABRAHAM'S BOSOM,

Luke 16.22 f.; also John 1.18). The passover meal was eaten in a reclining posture, and thus St John is here supplying evidence for St Mark's view of the supper rather than his own (see note on 13.1 above).

one of his disciples, whom Jesus loved

The mysterious figure of the 'Beloved Disciple' meets us here for the first time (cf. also 19.26; 20.2; 21.7, 20). St Mark (14.17) does not explicitly state that none but the Twelve was present at the supper, though perhaps that is implied. In view of St John's frequent liberties with the traditional material it cannot be regarded as at all certain that he thought of the Beloved Disciple as one of the Twelve, and indeed, if the 'other disciple' of 18.15 f. is to be identified with him, it is practically certain that he did not, since a Galilean peasant would be unlikely to have access to the residence of the high priest. Christian tradition from patristic times has identified the Beloved Disciple with St John himself, the son of Zebedee (Mark 1.19 f.) and the author of the Gospel. But the Fourth Gospel nowhere names the Beloved Disciple, and it would be possible to hold that he was a Jerusalem follower, such as John Mark, and that it was he who wrote the Fourth Gospel, or at least supplied the material out of which it was written.

27. then entered Satan into him

See note on 6.70; cf. also 13.2; 17.12.

30. and it was night

Again we notice the deep symbolism of night and darkness in the Fourth Gospel; cf. 1.5; 3.2, 19; 9.4; 12.35, etc.

31. Now is the Son of man glorified

'Now' means 'this is the hour'—in which the culminating point of the life and mission of Christ is reached. It is signalled by the departure of Judas; the powers of

F

evil are making their last desperate throw. Cf. 12.23, 28; 17.1, 5.

33. as I said to the Jews

i.e. in 7.34 and 8.21. The theme of the 'going away' of Christ (at the Ascension) is elaborated in the next chapter.

34. a new commandment

The expression is found in I John 2.7 f.; cf. John 15.12, 17; I John 3.11, 23; 4.21; II John 5.

35. By this shall all men know

St John is intensely aware that the visible unity and harmony of the Church is the most potent factor in evangelism (cf. John 17.21, 23; I John 4.20).

37. I will lay down my life for thee

The boast of Peter in Mark 14.31 (IF I MUST DIE WITH THEE, I WILL NOT DENY THEE) is thus translated into characteristically Johannine language (cf. 10.11, 15, 17 f.; 15.13). The irony is that it is not Peter who lays down his life for Christ but Christ who lays down his life for Peter. Nevertheless, in the end St Peter *does* lay down his life for Christ (21.19).

XIV

THE GOING AWAY OF CHRIST
TO THE FATHER

14.1-31

The continuous discourse of Jesus in Chapters 14 to 17 re-presents St John's profound meditation upon the death, resurrection and ascension of Christ; the whole tremendous content of these three words is to be understood each time the Evangelist speaks of Christ's 'going' or 'going away'. This going away is Christ's 'glorification'. The discourse is written from the point of view of the Church which, taught by the Spirit, has now come to appreciate the meaning of those events which the disciples could not have understood at the time when they were happening. It is the substance of what Jesus tried to teach the uncomprehending disciples towards the close of his earthly life (e.g. Mark 10.32-45; 13.1-37), as the apostolic Church came to understand that teaching under the guidance of the Holy Spirit. It consists of the MANY THINGS which Jesus had still to say to his followers, but which they could not BEAR in the days of his flesh (John 16.12); now (in St John's view) he had revealed them through the Holy Spirit, who had come to guide the Church into all truth (16.13). Thus, we are not to think of the discourse as a more or less verbatim report of an address actually given by the historical Jesus to his disciples; yet on the other hand we must not think of it as a free composition or subjective imagining of St John's. St John regarded the truths which the Holy Spirit had taught the Church after Christ's ascension as the heart of the Christian revelation. He did not give the same kind of almost superstitious veneration to historical 'facts' as we so often are inclined to do; IT IS THE SPIRIT THAT QUICKENETH, THE FLESH (i.e. the 'mere' historical facts) PROFITETH NOTHING (6.63). The words which Christ has spoken through his Spirit in the Church, quickening into life the words of the historical Jesus, these words ARE SPIRIT AND ARE LIFE (ibid.). It is the Holy Spirit in the Church who brings into the living present all the things that the Jesus of history said and taught to his disciples (14.26). St John is not recording the words of the historical Jesus as a matter of objective historical reportage, for no one in the first century AD had any such conception of historical writing; he is recording the words of the historical Jesus as they were understood by the Spirit-guided mind of the apostolic Church. It is this Spirit-taught interpretation of the deeds and words of Jesus which constitutes the Christian revelation, and it is this interpretation which St John sets down in these chapters. Thus, what we have here is not free composition or subjective fancy; it is the truth taught by the historical Jesus as it was understood through the operation of the Spirit in the apostolic Church. This—in so far as it can be expressed in words at all—is what the revelation in Jesus Christ is. It is thus not surprising, when we reflect upon the matter, that St John does not distinguish carefully between the words of the historical Jesus and the words spoken by the Risen Lord through the Spirit in the Church, because his conceptions both of history and of revelation are quite different from ours. To him the words of the Risen Christ, spoken through the Spirit to a prophet in the Church, are just as 'inspired', just as mandatory and authentic, as any remembered words of the Jesus of history.

2. many mansions

Lit., ABIDING-PLACES, RV marg.; the Latin uses mansio, 'halting-place', 'lodging', 'inn'. Hence MANSIONS in our

EVV, which is so puzzling to modern ears. The phrase means that there is room and to spare for all the redeemed in heaven; cf. Luke 15.17, BREAD ENOUGH AND TO SPARE. The death of Jesus is not the unrelieved catastrophe that it looks; it is simply the going of Jesus to his Father's home, where he will make ready a home for his friends.

6. I am the way, and the truth, and the life

There are a number of I AM sayings in the Johannine literature (other than those without a predicate; see on 8.24), e.g. I AM THE DOOR, I AM THE GOOD SHEPHERD, etc. cf. John 6.35, 51; 8.12, 23; 10.7, 9, 11, 14; 11.25; 14.6; 15.1, 5; Rev. 1.8; 2.6; 22.16). It has been suggested that they are utterances spoken by the Risen Christ through his Spirit to a prophet in the congregation and subsequently accepted by the Church as an authentic word of the Lord. It has also been noted that these 'I-sayings' are in content very similar to the self-testimony of Wisdom in the Wisdom literature of the OT and Apocrypha (e.g. Prov. 8.2, 14). The expression THE WAY in the NT is drawn from the vocabulary of sacrifice, although to most Anglo-Saxon minds it is simply an ethical term ('the way of Jesus' means the Sermon on the Mount for most of us). It means that in Christ we have our access to the Father (cf. Eph. 2.18; Heb. 9.8; 10.20), and that, though sinners, we may approach him with our acceptable offerings. Christ is our high priest who offers for us the gifts which we would not have been worthy to bring to God; he brings us into the holy presence of God. Cf. also Acts 9.2; 19.9, 23; 22.4. For Christ as THE TRUTH see John 1.4, 17; and for Christ as THE LIFE see 1.4; 4.10; 10.10.

no one cometh to the Father but by me

The saving knowledge of God comes only through Christ, for he is the *only* way to the Father; cf. Matt. 11.27; Luke 10.22; John 1.18; 6.46; 8.19; 17.25; Acts 4.12.

9. he that hath seen me hath seen the Father

The miracle of Christ is that he has enabled men with the eyes of faith to see the invisible God, to know the transcendent source of all being. Cf. John 12.45; I John 4.12, 20; Col. 1.15; Heb. 1.3.

11. believe me for the very works' sake

The meaning is: if the words of Christ fail to convince anyone of his unity with the Father, then the miracles ('works') which he has performed should do so, on the grounds stated by Nicodemus in 3.2: NO MAN CAN DO THESE SIGNS THAT THOU DOEST, EXCEPT GOD BE WITH HIM. Cf. 5.32 (and note above); 5.36; 9.32 f.; 10.21.

12. greater works than these shall he do; because I go . . .

This is not a crude assertion that believers will be able to work more spectacular miracles than those of Jesus himself. It is a prediction that, after Christ's ascension and because of it (BECAUSE I GO TO THE FATHER), the Church through the power of the Spirit will be enabled to continue Christ's work of opening the blind eyes, healing disease, forgiving sins, bringing life and feeding mankind with the living bread (the Eucharist), on a far greater scale than was possible when Christ's presence was localized in the flesh and subject to all the limitations of time and place. Christ's work was restricted and confined until he was set free from the constraint of his incarnate existence (cf. Luke 12.50).

13. whatsoever ye shall ask in my name

Christians are to pray only for things which they can ask in Christ's name, a condition which at once rules out all selfish petitions. Those prayers will be granted which are in accordance with God's will as revealed to us in Christ. Thus, Jesus is not making a kind of 'blanket' promise, that whatever we ask will be given us; he is saying that only the prayers that are in harmony with the divine will are of any avail. All Christian prayer is reducible to the single petition, THY WILL BE DONE. Cf. the prayer of Jesus himself, NOT WHAT I WILL, BUT WHAT THOU WILT (Mark 14.36).

16. another Comforter

The Greek word is *paraklētos*, an 'advocate', 'helper'; it is parallel to the Latin *advocatus*, one 'called in' to help or advise, esp. the counsel for the defence in a court of law. This sense is implied in the present context (I WILL PRAY THE FATHER); and in I John 2.1 (the only use of the word in the NT outside the Fourth Gospel) it is explicitly stated that WE HAVE A *paraklētos* ('intercessor'; RV, 'ADVOCATE') WITH THE FATHER, JESUS CHRIST THE RIGHTEOUS. Jesus Christ, risen and ascended, is our advocate with the Father in heaven; and he (or the Father) sends to us here below ANOTHER PARACLETE, namely, the Holy Spirit. The word 'Comforter', so misleading to modern ears, was fathered upon EVV by Wycliffe, for whom it meant *confortator*, i.e. 'strengthener', rather than 'consoler'. The idea of the Risen Christ as our heavenly intercessor appears explicitly in Rom. 8.34; I Tim. 2.5, and Heb. 7.25 (cf. 9.24), as well as in I John 2.1 (cf. also John 14.26; 15.26; 16.7). See note on the Holy Spirit in the Fourth Gospel at the end of this section (pp. 171-3 below).

17. the Spirit of truth

The expression occurs also at 15.26 and 16.13. It means 'the Holy Spirit who reveals the truth about Christ,' or, more simply still, 'who reveals Christ the truth' (cf. 14.26; 16.13). The sole function of the Spirit is to witness to Christ (16.13), and he bears this witness in the hearts of believers only; the world is totally ignorant of him.

he abideth with you, and shall be in you

In St John's view the indwelling Spirit is the *mode* of Christ's dwelling in his disciples after the ascension; hence

it is a matter of indifference to say ' he will come to you ' or
I COME UNTO YOU (v. 18). Christ comes to his disciples in
the coming of the Spirit (see note on the Holy Spirit below).

18. desolate
The Greek word is *orphanoi* (RV marg.), which means
' fatherless ' (as at James 1.27, its only other use in NT), or,
more generally, ' bereaved '.

20. The mutual ' abiding ' of the Son in the Father, the
Church in the Son and the Son in the Church, is one of the
great themes of the Fourth Gospel; it is developed in the
allegory of the True Vine in the next chapter.

22. Judas (not Iscariot)
A Judas, son of James, is mentioned only in the Lucan
lists of the apostles (Luke 6.16; Acts 1.13). He is tradition-
ally identified with Thaddaeus of Mark 3.18 and Matt. 10.3;
but conjecture on this topic is profitless.

thou wilt manifest thyself unto us, and not unto the world
The knowledge of Christ through the Spirit in the Church
is incomprehensible to THE WORLD in the sense of the world
that is alienated from God (see note on 1.10). In this age
the revelation in Christ is a mystery of faith; it cannot be
' made public ' by advertising techniques. Only God can
open the blind eyes; only the Holy Spirit can convince us
of the truth of Christ. The question also probably refers to
the fact that the resurrection appearances of the Lord were
made only to the personal disciples of Christ; why was not
the Risen Christ revealed to THE WORLD? No answer is
given, at least explicitly; indeed, Judas's remark is more
in the nature of a comment on the actual state of affairs
than a question demanding an answer. The revelation of
Christ to the world would be made in God's good time,
i.e. at the parousia (Rev. 1.7).

23. we will come unto him

The principle is again illustrated that in the activities of any one member ('person') of the Divine Trinity both the other members are also operative. See introductory note to 5.19-47 above. This follows from that mutual 'indwelling' ('co-inherence') of Father, Son and Holy Spirit.

26. the Holy Spirit, whom the Father will send in my name

The full title THE HOLY SPIRIT occurs only here in the Fourth Gospel (at 20.22 there is no definite article). The Father sends the Spirit here and at 14.16 (as in Luke 24.49; Acts 2.33), but in 15.26 and 16.7 it is the Son who sends the Spirit (cf. 20.22). We have thus another illustration of the principle mentioned in the previous comment. The Spirit comes *in the name* of Christ, i.e. as Christ's envoy or representative—we might even say as his *alter ego*.

he shall teach you all things

St John knows that it was only in the light of the Spirit's teaching after the ascension of Christ that the disciples came to understand the real meaning of what the historical Jesus had said and done: cf. WHILE YET ABIDING WITH YOU, i.e. in the flesh, v. 25. Christ's revelation was not completed by the historical Jesus but by the Spirit of the ascended Christ in his Church.

27. Peace I leave with you

PEACE was the word of farewell or of greeting (cf. John 20.19, 21, 26). Here it is spoken as a priestly blessing (cf. Num. 6.26), as at a solemn dismissal. Many have thought that the order of John 14-17 has been displaced and that these words (vv. 27-31) must originally have formed the conclusion of the whole discourse at the Supper. Certainly the last words of v. 31 would lead naturally to the opening words of 18.1.

not as the world giveth

The enjoyment of God's peace is not diminished by earthly strife or toil; it is of a different order from anything that THE WORLD understands by peace. Cf. Col. 3.15; II Thess. 3.16. The worst that the world can do, even the crucifixion of Christ, is no ground for despondency or fearfulness. The ' going away ' of Christ is no defeat but victory (cf. 16.33), and one in which the disciples participate by faith (cf. I John 4.4; 5.4).

28. The Father is greater than I

This saying must not be used (as it was, for instance, by the Arians of the fourth century AD) to establish dogmatic propositions concerning the inner structural relationships of the Trinity. St John is not thinking in such categories at all. The meaning is that the ultimate source of our confidence is in God's almighty power, more mighty in his works of salvation even than the stupendous signs wrought by Christ could have proclaimed. The Father is the ground and source of the whole Trinity, but the Son (cf. esp. John 10.30) and the Spirit are one with the Father in being (substance) and operation.

30. the prince of this world cometh

See note on 12.31; the HOUR of the prince of darkness is at hand (Luke 22.53; John 16.4).

he hath nothing in me

Satan has power over THE WORLD, which has been made subject to him; but Christ is NOT OF THIS WORLD (cf. 17.11; 18.36) and is not subject to his reign. There is no part of his being, not even his flesh, upon which Satan can fasten.

31. Arise, let us go hence

See note on v. 27 above.

NÓTE ON THE HOLY SPIRIT IN THE
FOURTH GOSPEL

It will be convenient to gather into a single note the teaching of St John concerning the Holy Spirit. In common with the rest of the NT he holds that the promised pouring out of the Spirit in the days of the Messiah (Joel 2.28 f.; Isa. 32.15; Ezek. 39.29; Zech. 12.10) has been fulfilled as a result of the death, resurrection and ascension of Jesus Christ. It was in order that this *dénouement* might take place that Jesus had to GO AWAY: IF I GO NOT AWAY, THE PARACLETE WILL NOT COME UNTO YOU (John 16.7). It is equally true to say either that the Father sends the Spirit (14.16, 26) or that the Son sends the Spirit (15.26; 16.7), because in the works of the Father the Son is active and *vice versa*. The Spirit proceeds from the Father (15.26) as indeed also does the Son (8.42; 13.3; 16.27 f., 30; 17.8); but St John uses a different word for the 'going forth' of the Spirit from the word by which he usually expressed the 'coming forth' of the Son. This emphasizes the truth that the mission of the Spirit is not identical with that of the Son and is indeed dependent upon the latter; the Spirit could not be given until Jesus's work in the flesh was finished (7.39). Thus, while it is nowhere stated that the Spirit 'proceeds' from the Son as he proceeds from the Father (and the Eastern Orthodox Church is right, as against the West, in the matter of the added *filioque* in the Nicene Creed), it is nevertheless shown that the Spirit issues from Christ and his finished work, as water issues from a fountain (7.37 f.); and this truth is expressed pictorially in the manner in which Christ *breathes* the Spirit upon his disciples after his resurrection (20.22; see note below). As God comes to the world in the coming of Christ, so Christ comes in the coming of the Spirit. The Spirit is the Spirit of

the risen Christ, the means by which his living presence
may be appropriated by his disciples in every place. For
St John the two expressions I WILL SEND . . . THE SPIRIT
and I WILL COME AGAIN (cf. 14.3, 18, 28) are different ways
of saying the same thing; the Spirit is the mode of Christ's
presence in his Church in the age between his resurrection
and his parousia. As in the rest of the NT, the Spirit is
thought of as the eschatological reality of Christ, appre-
hended only by faith, which is given to us in this period of
waiting for the return of Christ, i.e. the parousia. It is quite
untrue to suggest (as was frequently done in recent times)
that for St John the coming of the Spirit *was* the parousia,
the only form of the Second Coming that he recognized. It
was thus claimed that St John had 'de-eschatologized' the
Christian proclamation. There is, of course, no trace of
such notions in the Fourth Gospel. For St John, as for St
Paul, the Spirit in the Church was the EARNEST and FIRST-
FRUITS, vouchsafed to believers in the days of waiting, by
which they knew the certainty of the revelation of Jesus
Christ in his unveiled glory at his parousia (cf. Rom. 8.23;
II Cor. 1.22; 5.5; Eph. 1.14); in this age Christ is known
not to the world but only to believers by faith (John 14.17,
22) through the activity and in the mode of the Holy Spirit.
But at the parousia, at what St John calls THE LAST DAY
(6.40, etc.), Christ will be made manifest, not under the
veiled form of the Holy Spirit, but in his visible glory; and
EVERY EYE shall see him, no longer only the eyes of faith
(Rev. 1.7). Thus, we must not think of the Holy Spirit as a
personality that is quite separate and distinct from the
personality of Christ; the word 'person' in the ancient
creeds does not mean 'personality' in the modern sense.
For St John, as for the NT writers generally, the Holy
Spirit is Christ's *alter ego*, the form of his manifestation in
the Church in the period that will supervene before 'the
revelation' of Christ in glory, when we shall see him EVEN
AS HE IS (I John 3.2).

The function of the Holy Spirit is closely related to the two distinctively Johannine titles, PARACLETE and SPIRIT OF TRUTH. As Paraclete he is our present helper in this life, just as the Risen Christ is our ADVOCATE WITH THE FATHER in the realm above (I John 2.1; cf. Rom. 8.26 f.; see note on 14.16 above). As Spirit of truth he has a five-fold function. (1) He is ' with us for ever ' (14.16), representing Christ to us and in us (14.17); FOR EVER is literally ' unto the age ' i.e. the consummation of all things at the parousia (cf. Matt. 28.20). (2) He guides the disciples into ALL TRUTH, bringing home to them the true meaning of all that the Jesus of history had said and done (14.26; 16.13). (3) He bears witness to Christ; he does not testify to himself, but bears testimony to Christ alongside the testimony of the disciples in the world (15.26 f.; 16.14; cf. Mark 13.11). (4) He convicts THE WORLD OF SIN, OF RIGHTEOUSNESS AND OF JUDGMENT (see note below on 16.9-11). (5) Lastly, he declares to the Church THE THINGS THAT ARE TO COME (16.13): that is to say, he speaks through the prophets concerning the events that shall happen before and at the end of the world, after the manner of the ' revelation ' of ' John the Seer ' in the Apocalypse (Rev. 1.1).

XV

THE TRUE VINE

15.1-27

The representation of Israel under the form of a vine, vineyard, fig-tree or olive (the metaphor varied amongst these figures) was common in the OT and in contemporary Judaism. J. H. Bernard (ICC, II 478) has pointed out that when in the OT Israel is symbolized by a vine, her degeneracy is being lamented or her destruction foretold (cf. Ps. 80.8-16; Isa. 5.1-7; Jer. 2.21; Ezek. 15.1-8; 19.10; Hos. 10.1 f.; cf. also Rev. 14.18 f.). The Synoptists record that Jesus himself used this kind of imagery in his teaching (Matt. 20.1-16; 21.28-32; Mark 12.1-12; Luke 13.6-9); the enacted parable of the Barren Fig-tree belongs to the same cycle of metaphor (Mark 11.12-14, 20-25). Jesus had taught that Israel was a vine (or vineyard, etc.) which yielded a poor harvest in spite of all the loving care which God had lavished upon it. St John here reflects upon this Synoptic theme and draws out a special and distinctive lesson from it: Christ, not Israel, is the vineyard of God's planting, and all the OT sayings about vines, etc., are fulfilled, not in Israel, but in Christ. The vine(yard) of Israel has been rejected as worthless (cf. Mark 11.14); Israel indeed is a barren fig-tree (or vine); Christ is the *true* vine. St John still further develops the metaphor (perhaps we may compare Rom. 11.16-24). The vine becomes a figure of 'the whole Christ', the head and the members; it is the Johannine equivalent of the Pauline metaphor of the Body of Christ. The branches yield fruit only if they draw their life from the vine; if they are cut off, they are fit only for burning. The allegory teaches the essential unity of the Church as something not merely desirable but indispensable (see notes on 17.11 and 21 below). A eucharistic significance is implied in the idea of the life of the vine, which the wine of the Eucharist mediates; Church unity in its essential and deepest sense is a eucharistic unity, a common sharing of the life of Christ, offered to us through his death: EXCEPT YE EAT THE FLESH OF THE SON OF MAN AND DRINK HIS BLOOD, YE HAVE NOT LIFE IN YOURSELVES . . . (John 6.53-6). Participation in the Church's one Eucharist was what distinguished the true disciples of Christ in every place from the numerous schismatic sects which claimed to be genuine disciples but which, as St Ignatius said before AD 110, 'abstain from Eucharist'. The setting of the allegory of the Vine amongst the discourses of the Last Supper strengthens the suggestion that such a eucharistic reference is intended. Church unity is not merely symbolized but is actually effected in the Eucharist.

1. I am the true vine

On the I AM of the saying see note on 14.6 above. As elsewhere in St John TRUE means 'real', 'essential'; cf. TRUE MEAT, TRUE DRINK, John 6.55, RV marg.

my father is the husbandman

The Greek word *geōrgos* means a working farmer, in this case a vine-dresser; cf. I Cor. 3.6-9. In the OT symbolism God is thus represented as the one who plants or tends the vine, etc; e.g. Isa. 5.1 f.; Jer. 2.21.

6. cast them into the fire

Cf. Ezek. 15.4; Matt. 13.40-42.

12. See note on 13.34; cf. 15.17.

13. Greater love hath no man

Cf. 10.11; the idea of FRIENDS, here introduced, is explained in the next two verses.

14, 15. Ye are my friends

Cf. the definition of the brethren, etc., of Jesus in Mark 3.35. There is a profound paradox here. FRIENDS are those who obey the commands of Christ. But it is *slaves* who must obey their lord's will. However, Christ does not treat his disciples as slaves, who must obey willy-nilly and without comprehension; he has admitted them into the counsels of the Father, so that now they may obey freely and with full understanding, not as slaves who obey because they must, but as friends who delight to do the pleasure of their Friend. The word SERVANTS in RV should be translated SLAVES (see RV marg.); see note on 13.16 above.

16. Ye did not choose me, but I chose you

The doctrine of the divine *election* runs through the whole Bible; it is not we who have chosen God, however real our choice may have seemed to us; God took the initiative at every step, and all our questing and striving are but our response to his prompting: WE LOVE, BECAUSE HE FIRST LOVED US (I John 4.19; cf. John 6.70; Mark 3.13, and note esp. v. 19 below).

whatsoever you shall ask the Father in my name

See note on 14.13; cf. 15.7.

18. If the world hateth you

In this passage St John is expressing in his own way the warnings which Jesus in the Synoptists has given concerning the persecutions which his followers must endure in the world (e.g. Mark 8.34-38; 10.39; 13.9-13, etc.); here, as there, the disciples must be neither surprised nor dismayed to find that THE WORLD hates them. The point of view of the NT is that the persecution of the Church is one of the 'signs of the End', which will continue throughout history until the consummation of all things. Christians must not expect better treatment than their Lord received. Cf. 16.33.

20. See John 13.16 above; cf. Matt. 10.24.

24. the works which none other did

i.e., Christ's miracles, which are unique precisely because they are Christ's, the works of the Messiah. To have rejected the signs that the Age of the Messiah has arrived is the ultimate sin, which in the Synoptists is spoken of as BLASPHEMY AGAINST THE HOLY SPIRIT (Mark 3.29), when the mighty works of the Messiah had been ascribed to the power of Beelzebub.

25. written in their law

Here (as in 10.34) 'law' is not used in its restricted sense (the Pentateuch) but in its wider sense which includes the whole OT. The quotation is more probably from Ps. 69.4, a Messianic psalm, than from Ps. 35.19. The expression THEIR LAW does not mean that the OT is not a Christian book rather than a Jewish one; it means 'the Law of which they are so proud'; even their own Law condemns their hatred of Christ. Cf. also 8.17.

27. ye also bear witness

The Church's testimony is co-witness with that of the Holy Spirit (cf. Mark 13.11). The Spirit bears witness to Christ in the hearts of the disciples and they in their turn BEAR WITNESS THAT THE FATHER HATH SENT THE SON TO BE THE SAVIOUR OF THE WORLD (I John 4.14; cf. 1.2). The original apostles bear a uniquely historical witness to Christ, because they had been with him FROM THE BEGINNING of his ministry (cf. Acts 1.21 f.; 4.20).

XVI

'THE THINGS THAT ARE TO COME'

16.1-33

The Synoptic Gospels record that Jesus gave careful instruction to his disciples concerning the things that should happen between his death and his return in glory at the parousia (see esp. Mark 13 and parallels). He foresaw no easy triumph for the gospel; on the contrary the good news must be proclaimed amidst wars, earthquakes, famines and distress of nations. These were signs of the divine judgment, whereas the preaching of the good news was the sign of the divine mercy; together these things constituted the 'signs of the End'—evidences that we are living in the last period of world history before the consummation of all things at the parousia. The same truth is vividly represented in the Johannine Apocalypse, especially in the vision of the Four Horsemen (Rev. 6.1-8). Two particular features will characterize this end-period of history, namely, the persecution of the Church by the world and the activity of the Holy Spirit in the Church; they are well brought together in the words of Jesus in Mark 13.11: WHEN THEY LEAD YOU AND DELIVER YOU UP, BE NOT ANXIOUS BEFOREHAND WHAT YE SHALL SPEAK; BUT WHATSOEVER SHALL BE GIVEN YOU IN THAT HOUR, THAT SPEAK YE; FOR IT IS NOT YE THAT SPEAK, BUT THE HOLY SPIRIT. It is this saying in its setting that, as it were, forms the text of St John's meditation in Chapter 16 concerning THE THINGS THAT ARE TO COME (v. 13). In all the tribulations of this end-period of history, which shall overtake the apostles, they will bear their witness in the power of the Holy Spirit, secure in the joyful certainty that Christ has OVERCOME THE WORLD.

2. put you out of the synagogues
This, of course, had happened to the Christians at a fairly early date, and the breach between Church and Synagogue was complete soon after AD 70. Cf. John 9.22; 12.42.

4. Cf. John 13.19; 14.29. For THEIR HOUR see Luke 22.53.

7. It is expedient for you that I go away
While Christ is confined in bodily existence on the earth, the universal Spirit, which is under no such constraint, cannot begin the work of evangelizing all nations (cf. Mark 13.10; John 7.39).

8. And he, when he is come, will convict the world
The Spirit will work upon the conscience of the world not directly (14.17) but through the witness of the Church.

9. of sin
Through the Church's witness the world will be convinced of its own sinfulness, which is demonstrated by its unbelief. The whole Christian tradition has consistently held that unbelief is a sin and faith a virtue (see note on 8.21 above).

10. of righteousness
This Pauline word occurs only here (and v. 8) in the Fourth Gospel and we are made to think of the Pauline conception of Christ's death as a setting forth of the righteousness of God (Rom. 1.17; 3.25, etc.). The Holy Spirit will convince the world that the saving righteousness of God, proclaimed by the prophets of old, has now been active in the death, resurrection and ascension of Jesus Christ.

11. of judgment

The condemnation of Satan and his overthrow have been achieved by Christ's victory on the cross (cf. 12.31; 14.30; 16.33; see note on 12.31 above). This judgment upon Satan will convince the world of the certainty of the judgment that will fall upon itself.

13. he shall declare unto you the things that are to come

St John has all along stressed that during the lifetime of the historical Jesus his disciples did not understand the meaning of his person and work. It was only after his 'going away' and through the guidance of the Spirit that comprehension came to them. The early Church understood one of the functions of the Spirit to be to give warning concerning coming events (e.g. Acts 21.11). The Spirit spoke through the Church's prophets to shew them THE THINGS WHICH MUST SHORTLY COME TO PASS (Rev. 1.1; 22.6); and visions of the future, of the kind which we find in the Book of Revelation, are what St John has in mind when he says that the Spirit will declare coming events.

16. again a little while and ye shall see me

The primary reference, of course, is to Christ's resurrection appearances, but there is doubtless also a reference to Christ's coming to his disciples in the coming of the Holy Spirit (cf. 14.18 f., 28). Some have said that this is the only form of the 'Second Coming' that St John knows (e.g. J. A. T. Robinson, *Jesus and his Coming*, 1957, pp. 175 f.), but this view implies that his thought must be sharply distinguished from that of the Apocalypse: BEHOLD, HE COMETH WITH THE CLOUDS . . . (Rev. 1.7). It must also probably be distinguished from that of the 'Appendix'; cf. John 21.22, IF I WILL THAT HE TARRY TILL I COME. More probably St John held that Christ's coming with the Paraclete was a veiled appearing (cf. 14.22), and that his unveiled 'coming' would take place at the parousia, when EVERY EYE would see him. This is the usual NT view.

21. A woman when she is in travail hath sorrow

The arrival of the 'day of the Lord' is thought of in Judaism as a time of affliction, and is spoken of as the birth-pangs of the Messianic Age (cf. Isa. 13.8; 66.7-9; Nahum 2.10; Rev. 12.2). It seems to have been distinctive of the teaching of Jesus that the 'woes of the Messiah' were to fall, not upon his enemies, but first of all upon the Messiah himself; the 'woes' predicted in Mark 13 are fulfilled upon Jesus himself in the passion story and then upon his Church, the suffering remnant of Israel. (See R. H. Lightfoot, *The Gospel Message of St Mark*, 1950, pp. 48-59.) This conception is thoroughly understood by St John. THE HOUR of Israel's travail is THE HOUR of Christ's lifting up upon the cross, and Christ himself with his disciples is the bearer of the woes of the Messiah. But when the travail is accomplished, the joy of the Messianic community is boundless and enduring. (See also note on 19.5 below.)

23, 24. See note on 14.13 above.

25. 'Proverbs' means 'cryptic utterances'; see note on 10.6 above.

29. Lo, now speakest thou plainly

In this verse and the next the disciples profess to have understood the full meaning of all that Jesus has taught them about THE THINGS THAT ARE TO COME; they do not realize that they cannot understand the truth until the Spirit is given to them. Jesus, they suppose, knows all things, and no one needs to ask him further questions because they all now know the course of coming events. But Jesus knows that as yet they neither truly believe nor understand (v. 31). They are confident that they will play their part, but Jesus knows that they will run away at the critical moment and leave him alone—alone save for the Father's presence with him (v. 32).

33. that in me ye may have peace

Cf. 14.27. It is characteristic of faith in Christ that it brings deep underlying peace even amidst all the tribulations and distractions of life in the world. The source of the Christian's courage (GOOD CHEER) is the knowledge that Christ has overcome the world and its PRINCE (cf. 12.31; 14.1, 27; I John 5.4 f.; Rev. 3.21; 12.11; also Rom. 8.37; I Cor. 15.57).

XVII

THE HIGH PRIESTLY PRAYER

17.1-26

Jesus's prayer in this chapter is called his 'high priestly prayer' because in it he consecrates himself as the atoning victim, offered in sacrifice to God, by which the sin of the world is taken away, a new covenant between God and man is ratified in his blood, and the Church is perfected into one in him. In point of fact only in the Epistle to the Hebrews is Christ called 'high priest' in the NT, but the idea of his self-oblation is everywhere present. St John conveys this truth in his own characteristic way. Just as he gives no account of the Transfiguration but shews us the whole earthly life of Jesus as transfigured and glorified, so he gives us no account of the institution of the Eucharist at the Last Supper but presents the whole earthly life of Jesus as the Christian paschal offering or eucharistic sacrifice. Just as in the Fourth Gospel Jesus does not go to his cross as a helpless sufferer to his martyrdom but rather as a king to his crowning, so also he goes to Calvary not as an unwilling victim to the altar but as a voluntary sacrifice whose joy is fulfilled in his deliberate act of self-oblation. Thus, St John stresses that Jesus is not merely the gift offered but the offerer, not only the victim but the sacrificing priest: I LAY DOWN MY LIFE . . . NO ONE TAKETH IT FROM ME, BUT I LAY IT DOWN MYSELF. I HAVE POWER TO LAY IT DOWN, AND I HAVE POWER TO TAKE IT AGAIN (10.17 f.). Christ is the Lamb of God (1.29 and note above), the sacrifice provided by God himself (Gen. 22.8) to make atonement for the world's sin. The words of this prayer in John 17 are the 'words of consecration' spoken by the High Priest, that is by Jesus himself, over his body and blood, now being offered and given for the life of the world. They form the 'Prayer of Consecration' in the eucharistic rite constituted by the earthly life and death of Jesus: after that death Christ, our High Priest, stands at the heavenly altar dispensing his body and blood, whereby the unity of his Church is created and maintained. Into his own offering he has incorporated his disciples; he offers them, their souls and bodies, along with himself, for all are made one with him in his glorification of the Father—not only those disciples who were his original apostles, but the Church of all ages and all places, all those who believe on Christ through the apostles' word (v. 20). Thus does St John present in his own way the truth which Jesus dramatized when on the night on which he was betrayed he took bread and made eucharist, and also the truth that the eucharistic bread which the faithful receive Sunday by Sunday is Christ's FLESH given FOR THE LIFE OF THE WORLD (6.51), by means of which they ABIDE in him and he in them (6.56) and finally are raised up AT THE LAST DAY (6.54).

1. lifting up his eyes to heaven

i.e. in the attitude of prayer; cf. 11.41; Mark 7.34. It may be that this action was specially associated with the consecration of the elements in the Eucharist (cf. Mark 6.41).

the hour is come; glorify thy Son

This is the moment to which the whole life of Christ has been pointing forward (see notes on 2.4; 12.23, 28). Jesus has glorified God by his utter obedience (v. 4); now God glorifies Jesus, i.e. re-invests him with the glory which was laid aside at the incarnation, the glory which Christ had with the Father before the creation of the world (v. 5). The cross is the instrument of Christ's glorification.

2. thou gavest him authority over all flesh

Ps. 8 was interpreted Christologically in the early Church; see Heb. 2.5-8. The authority over all flesh, lost by Adam, is regained for Man in the person of the Son of Man (cf. Matt. 28.18; Rev. 2.26 f., etc.) and will be manifested in the exercise of judgment by the Son (John 5.27).

3. And this is life eternal

The knowledge of God mediated through Christ is even now in this age our first instalment or earnest of the life of the Age to Come (see note on 3.15 above).

4. having accomplished the work

This clause looks forward to the completed work of Christ acclaimed by the triumphant cry *tetelestai* (IT IS FINISHED) from the cross (John 19.30).

6. the men whom thou gavest me out of the world

St John regards Christian believers as the gifts of the Father to the Son; the Son guards them and keeps them in closest unity with the Father (cf. 6.37, 39; 10.29; 17.12; 18.9).

8. the words which thou gavest me I have given unto them

The earliest Christians guarded and treasured the words of Christ as a sacred tradition held on trust; St John obviously has the highest respect for this tradition of the words of the Lord, which he thinks of as having been imparted to Christ by the Father. The WORDS here referred to are doubtless those of the historical Jesus, whether those of the oral tradition or those of the written records; they are to be distinguished from the words of the Risen Christ spoken through the Spirit. On the whole question of the place of the tradition of the words of the Lord in the early Church see H. Riesenfeld, *The Gospel Tradition and its Beginnings*, 1957. Cf. also 8.26; 12.49; 15.15; 17.14.

9. I pray not for the world

It is not meant that Jesus is concerned only with the small company of the elect and not with the world (cf. 3.16; 4.42; 12.47); the sense of the Greek is, 'I am not now praying for the world but for those . . .' When THE WORLD is saved it ceases to be THE WORLD and becomes the Church.

11. that they may be one, even as we are

The prayer THAT THEY MAY BE ONE is repeated in vv. 21 and 22. The unity of the Church is the result of the fact that Christians are kept in God's name (i.e. essential nature) and partake of the glorification of Christ (v. 22). It is a sharing of the oneness which exists between Christ and the Father, a being caught up into the unity of the Godhead. Thus, Church unity is not merely a desirable feature of Christian existence; it is its *sine qua non*. It is not something which men can create, for God gives it; nor can they destroy it. What, alas, they can do is to obscure it.

12. the son of perdition

This is a Jewish title for Antichrist (cf. II Thess. 2.3), applied here (perhaps dramatically and poetically) to Judas Iscariot. See notes on 6.70 and 13.18.

15. The words are reminiscent of the two last clauses of the Lord's Prayer: BRING US NOT INTO TEMPTATION, BUT DELIVER US FROM THE EVIL ONE (Matt. 6.13). Jesus does not praise a 'fugitive and cloistered virtue'; his disciples will be sent into the world on their apostolic mission.

17. Sanctify them in the truth

In 10.36 it was said that Jesus was SANCTIFIED AND SENT INTO THE WORLD by the Father. So Christ will sanctify and send his disciples into the world (v. 18; also 4.38; 20.21). The word 'sanctify' means 'consecrate' (RV marg.) or set apart for a special function or task, usually priestly (e.g. Ex. 28.41) but not necessarily so (e.g. Jer. 1.5). Here it is probable that what is intended is a consecrating of the apostles for their part in the priestly and prophetic mission of Christ to the world after his ascension (cf. Rev. 1.6, he MADE US . . . PRIESTS UNTO HIS GOD AND FATHER; also Rev. 5.10; 20.6). They are to be consecrated in the truth of Christ—perhaps in the service of the truth of Christ.

19. And for their sakes I sanctify myself
   Christ is consecrated or is made priest on behalf of his people; he offers for them the sacrifice which they, being sinful, cannot offer on their own behalf. But the sacrifice itself is also consecrated that it may be holy to God and efficacious for its purpose of covering sin. Christ therefore consecrates himself both as priest and as victim. By his act of consecration his disciples are sanctified in him, so that they as priests may now themselves approach God and bring to him their acceptable sacrifices. This truth is symbolized in the Church's Eucharist. See note on 14.6 (THE WAY).

20. It is made quite clear that what is said in this chapter refers not merely to the original apostles of Jesus but also to all those in later generations who have believed the apostolic gospel.

21. that the world may believe that thou didst send me
   If we took the Bible quite seriously, it would be very clear that the primary reason for the Church's failure to evangelize the world was the fact of her disunity. In this verse and in v. 23 it is insisted that the gospel of the Incarnation and of the love of God cannot be effectively preached to the world by a disunited Church.

24. thou lovedst me before the foundation of the world
   THE FOUNDATION OF THE WORLD is a Jewish expression

XVIII

THE PASSION STORY

18.1 – 19.42

The passion story was the earliest part of the Gospel tradition to receive fixed shape; it is noteworthy that all four canonical Gospels tell the story with relatively slight divergences of matter and manner. This is true even of St John, whose passion story is the only part of his narrative, except 6.1-21, which follows the recognizable Synoptic pattern. His more important divergences are pointed out in the notes below. There is no good reason to suppose that he is in possession of a tradition unknown to the Synoptists. His own theological insights are responsible for such modifications as he introduces into the traditional material. His most striking emphasis—which is by no means absent from the Synoptists—is upon the fact that Jesus is from beginning to end in command of everything that happens; he is forced to do nothing which he does not will; Pilate and the rest are mere puppets in the story, acting a part which has been written for them; and Jesus majestically fulfils the divine purpose which he has come to fulfil, namely, to lay down his life and to offer his flesh for the salvation of the world. He comes to his cross like a king to the throne of the whole earth, or like a priest to the altar upon which he is to offer the one, full, perfect and sufficient sacrifice and oblation for the sins of the whole world.

THE ARREST OF JESUS

18.1-14

1. the brook Kidron

i.e. the winter-torrent (Arabic, *wadi*) that had to be crossed between the city and the Mount of Olives (cf. II Sam. 15.23; I Kings 15.13, etc.). We may ask why only St John mentions the brook which the party had to cross. Is it because he knew the site so well that he automatically mentioned the name? Or is this an instance of the tendency of the later tradition to give names to people and places not mentioned in the earlier tradition (e.g. Malchus, v. 10)? Or did St John see a parallel here with the withdrawal of David from Jerusalem when the forces of evil were gathering against him into the city (II Sam. 15.23)? Our answer to questions of this kind will depend on the view we have formed of the purpose of the Gospel and the character of its author. On the other hand, St John does not name Gethsemane, which he refers to as a GARDEN (cf. 19.41), whereas the Synoptists have spoken of it as a private farmholding (Mark 14.32; Matt. 26.36, RV margs.).

3. the band of soldiers

The Synoptists do not suggest that Roman soldiers were employed at the arrest—an improbability since Pilate had not yet been approached. The Greek word normally means COHORT (RV marg.), which consisted of 600 men, but St John may not imply that more than a detachment had turned out.

4. Throughout the Gospel St John has insisted on the supernatural knowledge of Jesus (e.g. 1.47; 4.18; 13.1, 21-27, etc.); he is not taken by surprise at the course of events after the Supper.

6. they went backward, and fell to the ground

The power of the mysterious I AM (see notes on 6.20 and 8.24 above) reveals itself strikingly. Jesus could not have been arrested had he not willed it.

8, 9. Jesus commands that his disciples be set free, thus fulfilling his own prophetic word in 17.12.

10. Simon Peter . . . cut off his right ear

It is characteristic that as tradition develops details are added. The Synoptists did not name either Peter or Malchus; Matthew and Mark did not say that it was the right ear, and St Luke alone adds that the ear was miraculously healed. There seems to be no allegorical significance in the name of Malchus, which is derived from the Hebrew *melek*, king; cf. the name 'Basil' from the Greek.

11. There seem to be clear references to Matt. 26.52 (which has no parallels in Mark and Luke) and to the prayer of Jesus in Gethsemane concerning the cup (Mark 14.36). Otherwise St John's passion narrative makes no allusion to Christ's Agony in Gethsemane, but we may recall the probable allusion in 12.27 (see note above).

12. the chief captain

The *chiliarch* (lit., 'captain of a thousand') was an officer in the Roman army (Latin, *tribunus*) and would command a cohort (cf. Acts 21.31). See note on v. 3 above.

13. Caiaphas, which was high priest that year

For Annas and Caiaphas, and for this phrase, see note above on 11.49. Caiaphas's counsel, mentioned in v. 14, was reported in 11.50.

AT THE HIGH PRIEST'S HOUSE

18.15-27

At first sight it might seem surprising that St John omits so much of the vivid narrative of St Mark at this point—the legal procedures described in Mark 14. 53-64, Jesus's claim to be Messiah and Son of Man (14.61 f.), and his condemnation as a blasphemer (14.64). But upon reflection it is clear that St John had no alternative. The Marcan account turns upon the production of his trump-card by the high priest after the disagreement of the witnesses, namely, the secret information that Jesus considered himself to be the Messiah. But in the Fourth Gospel Jesus has from the beginning publicly claimed to be Messiah, Son of God, Son of Man, etc., and has made no secret of his identity, as indeed Jesus himself asserts in John 18.20. Some re-writing of the tradition was therefore required at this point. It is not necessary to assume that St John is following a tradition that is independent of the Synoptic material.

15. Now that disciple was known unto the high priest

The story of Peter's denial is told by St Mark (14.54, 66-72), with whose words there is close affinity in this passage. But the detail of the intervention of the OTHER DISCIPLE is peculiar to St John. It is natural to identify him with the 'Beloved Disciple' of John 13.23, but there is no conclusive evidence for the identification; in that case the beloved disciple could not be John the son of Zebedee, another Galilean fisherman who would be no more likely than St Peter to have access to the high priest's house. Certainly some explanation of how Peter was admitted to the courtyard (COURT as in 10.1; see note above) of the house is called for, and it may well be that a Jerusalem disciple, perhaps a relative of the high priest, was instrumental in the matter. It may be that the statement of Polycrates (bishop of Ephesus towards the end of the second century AD) that St John was a priest and wore the priestly *petalon* is an inference from this verse.

19, 24. Perhaps the apparent confusion is to be explained by the fact that, though the Romans had officially made Caiaphas high priest, the Jews continued to treat Annas as if he had not been divested of the office (see note on 11.49 above). Thus Jesus is taken before Annas (v. 13), but it is necessary that Annas's verdict should be transmitted to Pilate by Caiaphas (v. 24).

27. straightway the cock crew
Peter's threefold denial is a precise fulfilment of the prophecy of Jesus in 13.38.

AT THE PRAETORIUM

18.28 – 19.16

St John's profound meditation upon the encounter between Jesus and Pilate must be read in the light of the great struggle between the Church and the Empire which was taking place at the time when he was writing. This struggle forms one of the main themes of the Book of Revelation; and, though there is a vast difference in the style of writing between the Johannine Gospel and Apocalypse, there is much common ground. (On this whole subject see E. Stauffer, *Christ and the Caesars*, Eng. trans. 1955, esp. pp. 147-91.) Both works embody the profound conviction that in some mysterious way the Roman Empire has a divinely appointed task and destiny, and that it could HAVE NO POWER . . . EXCEPT IT WERE GIVEN . . . FROM

G

ABOVE (John 19.11); it was GIVEN TO THE BEAST TO EXERCISE
AUTHORITY OVER EVERY TRIBE AND PEOPLE AND TONGUE AND
NATION (Rev. 13.7). Yet it is Christ, not Caesar, who is
WORTHY TO RECEIVE HONOUR AND GLORY AND BLESSING: it
is not THE BEAST (Caesar) but THE LAMB who is WORTHY TO
RECEIVE POWER AND RICHES AND WISDOM (Rev. 5.12 f.). In
the Praetorium Pilate appears to sit in judgment upon
Christ, but in reality it is Pilate who is judged before the
Son to whom all judgment has been given (John 5.22). The
trial scene before Pilate is permeated through and through
with the subtle Johannine irony, and 'jesting Pilate' speaks
unwittingly the profoundest words of truth: BEHOLD, THE
MAN! BEHOLD YOUR KING!

28. the palace
i.e. the PRAETORIUM (RV marg.), the 'residence' of the
Roman magistrate. Pontius Pilatus, procurator of Judaea
from AD 26 to 36, normally resided at Caesarea on the coast,
but came up to Jerusalem to keep order during the feasts.

they themselves entered not
Ritual uncleanness was incurred by entering the dwell-
ings of the Gentiles, and they wished to avoid having to
undergo the necessary rites of purification.

31. It is not lawful for us
John takes for granted the traditional account that Jesus
has been pronounced worthy of death (Mark 14.64); he has
not reported the condemnation by the Jewish court.
Whether in fact St John is right in saying that the Jewish
authorities could not carry out a capital sentence is much
debated by scholars; see C. K. Barrett, pp. 445 f.

32. by what manner of death he should die
The reference is to 12.32 f.; the point is that if the death
sentence had been carried out by Jews, Jesus would have

been stoned (cf. John 8.59; 10.31; Acts 7.58 f.); but Jesus had prophesied that he would die by crucifixion, the Roman form of capital punishment for malefactors of subject races.

35. Am I a Jew?
All the intensity of racial hatred, as felt by the proud Roman for the despised Jew, lies behind this question.

36. My kingdom is not of this world
'Kingship' or 'reign' is a better translation of *basileia*: 'Mine is not a worldly sovereignty,' in competition with political authority on the earth, such as that of Rome. The word is not common in the Fourth Gospel; see note on 3.3.

37. Thou sayest that I am a king
The translation of RV marg. here is not to be preferred. As in Mark 15.2 the answer of Jesus means, 'You have said it, not I.' But St John adds a characteristically Johannine affirmation of what the kingship of Jesus involves: Israel's Messianic King has come from God to witness to the truth. But Pilate understands the meaning of neither kingship nor truth. If he did, he would see that Jesus is the true king, not of the Jews only, but of all the world. 'Kingship' is a most important category in Johannine thought, and it is noteworthy that Jesus's conversation with Pilate, the representative of earthly political sovereignty, turns entirely upon it. Behind St John's story of the trial of Jesus before Pilate there stands the vision of the kingdoms of the world having BECOME THE KINGDOM OF OUR LORD AND OF HIS CHRIST: AND HE SHALL REIGN FOR EVER AND EVER (Rev. 11.15).

38. I find no crime in him
As in the Synoptists, Pilate is made to testify to the innocence of Jesus. It is stressed in various ways that the

Jews, not the Romans, are primarily responsible for the death of the Messiah (Mark 15.9 f.; Matt. 27.19-25; Luke 23.13-22; John 19.11 f.). Cf. also 19.4 and 6.

39. ye have a custom
Cf. Mark 15.6-11. No evidence outside the Gospels has been found for this custom, but it is by no means an improbability. Note the offensive way in which Pilate makes his offer to the Jewish authorities, calling Jesus THE KING OF THE JEWS. The detail is from Mark 15.9.

40. Barabbas
St John greatly compresses Mark's narrative, and he presupposes prior knowledge of the tradition. He is content simply to describe Barabbas as a ' robber ', whereas in Mark 15.7 he is a dangerous insurrectionary, perhaps a political ' messiah '. Nevertheless St John's brevity is very telling and memorable. ' Barabbas ' (lit., ' son of the Father ') was a common Jewish name and we need look for no hidden meaning in it.

19. 1-4.
The details of the scourging, the buffeting by the soldiers, the purple robe, the crown of thorns and the mock-cheering are all from Mark 15.15-19. But now St John introduces one of his brilliantly conceived and dramatic presentations of the truth behind history; the shewing forth of Jesus, wearing the kingly insignia, to the waiting crowd outside the Praetorium. The soldiers thought they were being wittily ironical when they invested Jesus with the robe and crown, but the true irony of the situation was that the object of their mock-worship was in truth none other than the KING OF KINGS AND LORD OF LORDS, ARRAYED IN A GARMENT SPRINKLED WITH BLOOD and treading THE WINE-PRESS OF THE . . . WRATH OF ALMIGHTY GOD, whose NAME IS CALLED ' THE WORD OF GOD ' (Rev. 19.11-16).

5. Behold, the man!

A whole treatise is required on this saying. Adam (a Hebrew word meaning 'man') was created by God to be a king over the whole created world; all creation was to be ruled by a son of man (Hebrew, *ben adam*) (Ps. 8; see note on 17.2 above). In Christ, the Son of Man, God's original intention in the creation is fulfilled. He is the new Adam, the Messianic King. Thus, we have in Pilate's words a striking example of Johannine *double entendre*; whereas Pilate might merely have meant, 'Look, here is the fellow,' his words contain the deepest truth about the person of Christ. A parallel meaning will underlie his words in v. 14, 'BEHOLD, YOUR KING!' Perhaps some such undercurrent of meaning is implicit in John 16.21 (. . . JOY THAT MAN IS BORN INTO THE WORLD); the sorrows of Eve are swallowed up in the joy of Mary, the Second Eve.

6. Take him yourselves and crucify him

St John cannot mean that Pilate was serious in saying this (in view of 18.31); he must have meant, 'Do what you like with him; he is not a criminal in the eyes of Roman law.' To this the Jews reply that according to their Law (e.g. Lev. 24.16) Jesus should be executed as a blasphemer.

8. he was the more afraid

To a Roman the claim to be 'SON OF GOD' would be a direct challenge to the Emperor, who was *Divi Filius*; perhaps Pilate is afraid that the case is going to have political repercussions after all. But probably St John implies that Pilate was in the grip of a numinous fear as a result of his personal encounter with Jesus (cf. 18.6). This interpretation is supported by Pilate's next question, 'WHENCE ART THOU?'

11. Thou wouldest have no power

The significance of this pregnant utterance concerning

the source of political authority (RV marg.) has been dis-
cussed in the introductory note to this section. St Paul
advances the same view in Rom. 13.1-7.

12. Caesar's friend

The Jews have noticed that their most successful line
is to play upon Pilate's political fears; he cares little for
their laws about blasphemy.

13. and sat down on the judgment-seat

It is not clear from the Greek whether Pilate himself
sat on the judgment-seat or whether he caused Jesus to
sit upon it. The latter interpretation is supported by the
mocking irony of ' BEHOLD, YOUR KING! ' Perhaps (as C. K.
Barrett suggests, p. 453) St John is being deliberately
ambiguous, as so often: Pilate in fact sat on the judgment-
seat but in reality it was the Son of Man, to whom all
judgment had been given, who was sitting in judgment upon
the nations, Jewish and Gentile alike. Here, then, would
be another striking example of St John's double irony.

Gabbatha

St John gives a Greek and a Hebrew (i.e. Aramaic) name
for the place; the former is not a translation of the latter,
which is of doubtful derivation. If there is any theological
significance in the names, we do not know what it is. Nor
do we know where the place was.

14. Now it was the Preparation of the passover

The sixth hour was noon. The day was the eve of
Passover, which began at six o'clock on the evening of
what we would call the same day, but which for the Jews
was the beginning of the next day. On the conflict between
St John and the Synoptists about the date of the crucifixion
see note on 13.1 above. A further disagreement with the
Synoptic tradition is that, whereas here Jesus is delivered

to be crucified at noon, in Mark (15.25) Jesus is crucified at the third hour (9 a.m.) and at midday there is darkness over the whole land (15.33). St John, however, is not concerned with chronological accuracy and we need not suppose that he is following an independent tradition. His purpose is profoundly theological. Jesus is delivered to be crucified (though he has not been condemned) at the hour of the Preparation, i.e. the time when the passover lambs were selected and killed in readiness for the Feast in the evening. He is the Lamb of God, who takes away the sin of the world (1.29; cf. also 19.36).

15. We have no king but Caesar

HE CAME UNTO HIS OWN, AND THEY THAT WERE HIS OWN RECEIVED HIM NOT (John 1.11). The rejection of their messianic King by the chief priests of Israel is deliberate and total. They had joined in the worship of THE BEAST (Caesar) with ALL THOSE WHOSE NAMES ARE NOT WRITTEN IN THE BOOK OF LIFE OF THE LAMB THAT HATH BEEN SLAIN FROM THE FOUNDATION OF THE WORLD (Rev. 13.8).

XIX

THE CRUCIFIXION OF CHRIST

19.17-37

St John's account of the crucifixion follows St Mark's. His alterations are significant theologically rather than historically, and it is unnecessary to suppose that he is following an independent tradition.

17. bearing the cross for himself

St John omits all mention of Simon of Cyrene, doubtless in order to stress the truth that Jesus is the sole sin-bearer needing no assistance from any source. Perhaps he regarded Gen. 22.6 as a possible 'type' of Christ's bearing of the cross.

Golgotha

'Skull Place' is a translation of the Aramaic 'Golgotha'. We do not know how it acquired its sinister name or indeed where exactly it was located. The detail is from Mark (15.22), but the Marcan episode of the wine mingled with myrrh is omitted.

19. a title

This word is a Latinism (*titulus*), the technical name of the placard naming the condemned man and his crime. Mark calls it an epigraph (SUPERSCRIPTION). The wording on the board is substantially the same in all four Gospels. Pilate gives his sarcasm the widest publicity; according to St John (only) he uses three languages, and the chief priests duly lodge their protest.

22. What I have written I have written

Pilate remains utterly unconscious that his words uttered in jest are true in the deepest possible sense, and that what he has written had long ago been written in the Scriptures, that the Christ should suffer. Cf. Acts 13.27 f.

23. The soldiers . . . took his garments

St Mark (15.24) has recorded the casting of lots for the garments of Jesus, paraphrasing but not explicitly mentioning Ps. 22.18. St John quotes the verse in full, and he understands its parallelism to mean that one particular garment was not divided but gambled for. This was the COAT (RV marg., TUNIC) without a seam. Probably St John has in mind the seamless robe of the Jewish high priest (the *ephod*; Ex. 28.31 f.), which must not be rent (Lev. 21.10). The Law is unwittingly fulfilled by the soldiers: the seamless robe of our great High Priest is not torn, just as in vv. 33, 36 it is insisted that the bones of of our Paschal Lamb were not broken. St John believes that the soldiers (like Pilate) did what they did THAT THE SCRIPTURE MIGHT BE FULFILLED (v. 24). St Cyprian (died AD 258) may not have been far wrong when he said that the seamless robe symbolized the unity of the Church; cf. Hoskyns (p. 529), 'the indivisible robe, which is closely associated with the body of the Lord, may symbolize the unity of the believers who are joined to the Lord, and feed upon his Body, in contrast to the division of the Jews, who are torn into factions because of him.'

26. Woman, behold thy son!

St Mark (15.40 f.) records that the women who had come up with Jesus from Galilee watched the crucifixion FROM AFAR; he does not mention the Mother of the Lord specifically. That they should have watched *from a distance* is not at all unlikely. St John, however, is not thinking of historical probability but of theological significance. It is useless to ask whether the story is founded upon fact or why the brothers of Jesus should not have accepted their responsibilities (cf. Acts 1.14). St John's thought does not move on this level at all. The Beloved Disciple figures here precisely because he is unidentified and unidentifiable. He is the type of the new member of the family of God, which is brought into existence by Christ's death. The unity of the Church, of which the seamless robe is a symbol, is exhibited here as in a picture. The Mother of Jesus becomes the mother of all the faithful; she is the Second Eve, the mother of all who live in Christ; the Church is the womb of the recreated humanity of the Second Adam. Cf. the strange symbolism of Rev. 12.5 in its context, which doubtless arises from this 'Johannine' manner of thought. See also notes on 2.1 and 4 above.

27. from that hour

The lifting up of Christ on the cross is the hour of the Church's birth.

28. all things are now finished

In St John's view Jesus had all along been fulfilling a foreordained scriptural plan; he now brings about the fulfilment of the only scriptural prophecy that still remained to be accomplished, viz. Ps. 69.21: IN MY THIRST THEY GAVE ME VINEGAR TO DRINK. St Mark had recorded the incident of the vinegar in a sponge, but without explicitly alluding to the Scripture (15.36). St. John alters Mark's 'REED' to 'HYSSOP' (a small plant that grew in walls, much less useful for this purpose than a good, stout reed), doubtless because at Passover the lintels of the doors were sprinkled with hyssop dipped in the blood of the paschal lamb (Ex. 12.22). Christ is THE DOOR (John 10.9) now symbolically sprinkled at the Preparation.

30. It is finished
Lit., 'It has been accomplished.' See note on 17.4.

he bowed his head, and gave up his spirit
Cf. the wording of Mark 15.37; Matt. 27.50 (also Luke 23.46). It has been suggested that St John's *double entendre* is again at work; he modifies the traditional wording so as to suggest that Jesus *handed over* (the meaning of the Greek for 'GAVE UP') his Spirit (i.e. the Holy Spirit), to those towards whom he bowed his head. Now that Jesus was 'GLORIFIED', the Spirit could be given (cf. 7.39). But this interpretation is altogether improbable in view of the solemn imparting of the Spirit in 20.22. 'SPIRIT' here (as sometimes elsewhere in St John, e.g. 11.33) means the human spirit of Jesus.

31. bodies should not remain on the cross
According to the Law (Deut. 21.22 ff.) bodies should not be left hanging *at night*. Perhaps St John means, 'especially in view of the fact that the Sabbath would begin in a few hours (6 p.m.), and it was a "high Sabbath", namely, passover-day as well.' Since the Sabbath is Saturday, St John confirms the view that Jesus died on a Friday (cf. Mark 15.42). The breaking of the legs was a cruel method of hastening the death of men dying in agony.

34. there came out blood and water
When the soldier pierced Jesus's side (to make sure that he was dead), there came out blood and water. The symbolism is profound: from Christ's self-oblation there flow the healing waters of baptism and the life-giving blood of the Eucharist. A great number of Johannine texts spring at once to mind, e.g. John 4.14; 6.53-56; 7.37-39; 13.8; 15.3; I John 1.7; 5.6-8; Rev. 1.5; 19.13; 21.6; 22.1, etc.

35. he that hath borne witness
This verse is perhaps the most baffling in the whole

Gospel. Who is this mysterious witness? The Beloved
Disciple? We are not told so. And is it meant that he attests
the historical truth of the incident, or that a witness—any
Christian—who has experienced the saving laver of baptism
and been united with Christ in the Eucharist will know the
truth about Christ's saving death and will testify to it so
that others may believe also? Our answer to these questions
will depend upon the view which we have formed of the
Evangelist's intention and character. It may be remarked
that the incident of the breaking of the legs and lancing
of the side are not reported in the Synoptic tradition.

36. A bone of him shall not be broken
The Law decreed that a bone of the passover lamb must
not be broken (Ex. 12.46; Num. 9.12). The Scripture was
fulfilled in respect of the Christian Passover Lamb (cf.
I Cor. 5.7). Perhaps St John has also in mind Ps. 34.20,
which in its context is most appropriate in respect of the
suffering Messiah.

37. They shall look on him whom they pierced
The quotation is from Zech. 12.10, which again is not
inappropriate in its context. A different use is made of the
prophecy in Rev. 1.7.

THE BURIAL OF CHRIST

19.38-42

The Synoptic tradition records the burial of Jesus by
Joseph of Arimathaea, A COUNCILLOR OF HONOURABLE
ESTATE (Mark 15.43). Perhaps the apostolic Church saw
in the action the fulfilment of an OT 'type': Joseph had
begged permission of Pharaoh to bury the body of the old
Israel (Jacob) (Gen. 50.4-6). This may be why the name

of Joseph of Arimathaea has been preserved in the Gospel records. Nicodemus (cf. note on 3.1 above) nowhere appears in the Synoptics. We have already noted the divergence between St John and the Synoptists in the matter of the anointing of the body of Jesus for burial (see note on 12.1-11 above); we may note here that Mary Magdalene in John 20.1 is not said to have gone to the tomb to anoint the body (contrast Mark 16.1); Nicodemus has performed the office already, and he had not done it stintingly (v. 39). It is likely that the Evangelists record the part played by Joseph (and St John adds Nicodemus) in order to cite independent evidence—that, perhaps, of a Sanhedrin member—of the fact that Jesus *really* died, as against Gnostic theories of resuscitation and Jewish accusations of fraud on the part of the disciples.

41. in the garden a new tomb

Only St John says that Jesus was buried in a garden; see note on 18.1. But he seems to have taken the detail that no one had yet been laid in the tomb from Luke 23.53; cf. Mark 11.2.

XX

THE RESURRECTION AND ASCENSION OF CHRIST

20.1-31

It would seem that in his resurrection story St John as elsewhere makes use of traditional material but adapts it to his own purpose. He follows St Luke (24.12) in recording St Peter's visit to the tomb after it had been reported that it was empty, and he adds that the Beloved Disciple accompanied St Peter. Our view of whether St John had a separate source of information beyond the Synoptic materials will depend upon whether we think that the Beloved Disciple is an historical character or not. If he is, the silence of the Synoptists is hard to understand. It is perhaps easier to hold that St John has no separate historical tradition which the Synoptists did not know, and that here, as in the rest of his Gospel, he is bringing out the theological significance of the traditional material in his own way. Again he is setting forth the truth of history by means of stories which are not in their details intended to be literally true. The most striking feature of St John's resurrection story is that the ascension of Christ to the Father and the giving of the Holy Spirit take place on the day of resurrection itself. This brings St John into disagreement with the stylized Lucan account of the Forty Days and the giving of the Spirit at Pentecost (Acts 1.3; 2.1); but there are good reasons for thinking that it is St Luke who has presented his materials theologically rather than historically, since he wishes to shew that the giving

of the Law on Sinai at Pentecost was the 'type' foreshadowing the giving of the Spirit at Pentecost after Jesus
(like the first Moses, according to rabbinic tradition) had
been taken up ('assumed') into heaven. In other words
St John is reverting to a tradition of the resurrection, ascension and giving of the Spirit that is much older than St
Luke's highly literary and theological elaboration of the
material. The rest of the NT agrees with St John rather
than with St Luke in not distinguishing very precisely
between the resurrection and the ascension of Christ.

1. on the first day of the week
    i.e., Sunday. So Matt. 28.1; Mark 16.2; Luke 24.1. All
the sources agree that the tomb was discovered empty very
early in the morning. All the Synoptists agree that Mary
Magdalene was not alone. All four Evangelists agree that
the stone had been rolled away from the door of the tomb.
The Synoptists all agree that the women saw an angel or
angels; in St John the Magdalene does not see the angels
until after she has been away and returned (v. 12). The
Synoptists do not record an appearance of the Lord to
Mary Magdalene (except in St Mark's Longer Ending:
Mark 16.9).

Mary Magdalene
    She has been mentioned in John only at 19.25. In the
Synoptists she is mentioned only as a witness of the crucifixion and empty tomb—except at Luke 8.2 as one of the
women who had been healed by Jesus and who were with
him in Galilee. She must not be confused with Mary of
Bethany or with either of the women who anoint Jesus in
Mark 14.3-9 and Luke 7.36-50. See notes above on 11.1,
2 and 12.1-11.

5. he seeth the linen cloths lying
    St John seems to be elaborating his source, viz. Luke

24.12. Or are we to suppose that these circumstantial details were in fact supplied by a genuinely historical witness, the anonymous Beloved Disciple?

8. he saw and believed

This is characteristically Johannine language about 'seeing' and 'believing' (cf. esp. 20.29; also 9.36-41). In Luke 24.12 St Peter, after he has seen the empty tomb, goes away puzzled to his own home. Presumably St John here implies that, though St Peter had seen, he had not believed, whereas the Beloved Disciple is the first to believe in the resurrection and it is his faith rather than St Peter's which may claim the primacy (cf. Matt. 16.16 f.).

9. For as yet they knew not the scripture

i.e., they had not yet been guided by the Holy Spirit to understand the true interpretion of those scriptural texts which the Church later came to regard as prophecies of the resurrection of Christ, e.g. Ps. 16.10, etc. Cf. John 2.22.

16. Jesus saith unto her, Mary

The deeply moving story of the weeping Magdalene's encounter with her Lord in the garden of the resurrection illustrates in an utterly unforgettable way the personal nature of the relationship of the Risen Christ to his disciples. Jesus speaks her name, and Mary at once knows who he is. Are there any more poignant words in the Gospels than these? Could the truth of the believer's relation with the Lord be more adequately expressed in any other way? Cf. John 10.3: HE CALLETH HIS OWN SHEEP BY NAME.

Rabboni

Aramaic, 'master', 'teacher', the same word as 'rabbi', but somehow this form seems more personal. Cf. John 1.38; also Mark 10.51, where the same verbal form is used.

17. Touch me not; for I am not yet ascended

Mary sees Jesus after his resurrection from the tomb but before he has ascended to the Father. The ascension to the Father is the final stage of Christ's glorification, and the Gospel has all along been pointing towards it (3.13; 6.62; 7.33; 13.1, 3; 14.28; 16.17, 28; 17.13). The giving of the Holy Spirit cannot take place until Christ has gone to the Father (16.7). The imparting of the Spirit to the disciples in 20.22 shews that the ascension to the Father has now taken place. Thus, Mary is bidden not to touch the risen Christ because he is not yet ascended to the Father, whereas in v. 27 St Thomas is invited to touch the Lord with his finger and hand, to prove not merely that Christ is risen but that he is ascended. Mary is told to go to Christ's BRETHREN—i.e. the disciples—and tell them of his ascension to their common Father and God. It is hardly possible to doubt that St John is thus returning behind St Luke to the primitive tradition of the Lord's resurrection and ascension as essentially the same event in its twofold aspect. We (under St Luke's influence) tend to think of the bodily appearances of the risen Lord as having ceased with the ascension; St Paul (I Cor. 15.8) and St John did not do so. We must reflect very seriously that all attempts to state in human words the great mystery of our redemption by Christ's death and exaltation are only approximations to the truth that lies utterly beyond our comprehension, until the day when WE SHALL SEE HIM AS HE IS. The object of all the Gospel writers—the Synoptists as well as St John—is not as historians to tell us 'what happened', for the acts of God are mysteries which cannot be laid open to the inspection of the historian; their object is to witness to us, by preaching, by symbols, by a Gospel *story*, the miraculous acts of God for our salvation.

19. it was evening, on that day, the first day of the week

St John, it would seem, heavily emphasizes the fact that

Jesus, having ascended to the Father, imparted the Holy
Spirit to the Church on the day of resurrection itself. If
it was still the same day, it was not yet 6 p.m.

Jesus came and stood in the midst

The Gospels all emphasize the fact that the tomb in
which Jesus was buried was found empty, and therefore
by implication the physical resurrection of the Lord. St
John (following St Luke) has also emphasized the matter
by his elaboration of the detail of the grave-clothes (vv.
6 f.) There are no reasons whatever, either in modern
science or in modern philosophy, why we should not accept
the NT witness concerning the Empty Tomb. If we truly
believe that God performed the stupendous act of raising
Jesus from the dead, we will not quibble about how he could
or could not have done it. The bodily resurrection of the Lord
is theologically very important in shewing that the whole of
creation is to be redeemed, the physical no less than the
spiritual. Nevertheless, St John does not wish to leave us
with the impression that the body of Jesus was entirely
unchanged; it was the same body by which his disciples
had always recognized him, the body which bore the marks
of the nails and the spear; yet it was transformed, a glorified
body, for Jesus had now ascended to the Father. As usual
St John conveys deep theological truth in the form of a
story. Jesus came and stood in the midst, in his resurrection
body, although the doors were bolted FOR FEAR OF THE JEWS.
Thus, the body of Jesus was now different in some respects
from the body that hung on the cross; and yet it was the
same body, for that was how the disciples knew who he
was: HE SHOWED UNTO THEM HIS HANDS AND HIS SIDE
(v. 20). There is deep symbolic truth in the story, and it is
much more important that we should understand it than
that we should try to make theories about exactly 'what
happened' and just *how* such an event could have occurred.
If we are worrying about these things, we are in the con-

dition of Thomas in vv. 24 f. We cannot have 'proofs' and 'experimental verifications', because the acts of God must always remain mysterious to us. St John is much more concerned with the deep theological truth that he is teaching us in his story: at the ascension Jesus Christ did not lay aside his humanity, when he returned to THE GLORY which he had with the Father BEFORE THE WORLD WAS (17.5). At the Incarnation he had been made man, 'as never to be unmade more'; he had taken our human nature, as nevermore to lay it off. His return to his disciples in his glorified body is a profound symbol of this truth of Christ's ascension: he did not divest himself of the robe of the flesh which he had accepted from the Virgin Mary, when for our sakes he was made man (1.14); he carried our humanity to the Father's throne, that where he is we may even now be ascended with him in glory (cf. Col. 3.1-4).

Peace be unto you
   The phrase is the normal Jewish greeting, but St John would wish us to read into PEACE the content of 14.27 and 16.33.

21. As the Father hath sent me, even so send I you
   The risen Christ commissions his disciples for their task of continuing the mission to the world upon which the Father had sent the Son; that task is to gather mankind into the unity of the Father and the Son which constitutes the Church of Christ (cf. 17.18, 21-23; also 11.52); it is nothing less than to restore the unity of mankind, which was lost by Adam's fall at the first creation.

22. he breathed on them, and saith . . . Receive ye the Holy Ghost
   Again St John presents ineffable truth in a picture: Jesus breathes into the 'new creation', of which his Church is the eschatological anticipation, the breath of life,

as God breathed into the Old Adam the breath of life (cf. Gen. 2.7; also 1.2). (See note on 3.8 above.) The disciples are the EARNEST or FIRSTFRUITS (in Pauline terms) of that new heaven and new earth to which the whole redemptive process points forward (Rev. 21.1). The ascension has taken place; Christ is no longer incarnate upon earth; yet the TABERNACLE OF GOD IS WITH MEN, AND HE SHALL TABERNACLE WITH THEM (Rev. 21.3) through the coming of the Holy Spirit, until the day when Christ returns in visible glory and EVERY EYE SHALL SEE HIM (Rev. 1.7). The Church is henceforward upon the earth the tabernacle of God with men, or (if we care to use the phrase) 'the extension of the incarnation'. As such the Church is empowered to exercise divine authority on the earth, to forgive or to retain sins.

23. whose soever sins ye forgive . . .

This seems to be St John's version of the sayings of Christ recorded in Matt. 16.19 (to St Peter) and 18.18 (to THE DISCIPLES, 18.1). The NT writers had no doubt that Christ gave to his Church authority in the matter of men's eternal destiny (cf. also Luke 22.29 f.; I Cor. 5.4 f.). But this verse does not help us to answer the question whether this authority is given to the whole Church corporately or to a particular order or ministry within it. For St. John the Church is clearly an apostolic ('sent') Church, but he never refers to 'the apostles' as such. Here we have been told only that THE DISCIPLES were in the closed room and that they received the Spirit and the authority to forgive or retain sins. Does St John distinguish between THE TWELVE (v. 24) and a wider company whom he calls THE DISCIPLES (vv. 19, 20, 25, 26, 30)?

24. But Thomas . . . was not with them

For Thomas called Didymus see note on 11.16 above. This story, peculiar to St John, sums up in a picture his recurrent theme of 'seeing and believing'. It is possible to 'see' and yet not to believe, like the Jews who saw Christ in the flesh (9.41); the original disciples both saw and believed (cf. 20.8), though Thomas had declared that if he did not see he would not believe (20.25). But the point that St John is most eager to make is the blessing that rests upon all those Christian disciples who, though they HAVE NOT 'SEEN', YET HAVE BELIEVED the apostolic testimony (20.29; cf. 17.20; I John 1.1-3); and upon this note he ends his Gospel. It is these Christians for whom he is writing—that they may BELIEVE THAT JESUS IS THE CHRIST, THE SON OF GOD (20.31). Here, surely, is St John's own refutation of the suggestion that he wrote for thoughtful but uncommitted representatives of the 'higher paganism' or philosophical religion of the Hellenistic world.

27. Reach hither thy finger, and see my hands

In this final picture of his Gospel St John is powerfully presenting the truth which has underlain all his book: WHEN YE HAVE LIFTED UP THE SON OF MAN, THEN SHALL YE KNOW THAT I AM HE (8.28). It is in his death on our behalf that Jesus is made known to us as our Lord and God: the gospel of the cross is the power of God unto salvation. A Messiah who had not been lifted up would have no power to draw us to him. Like St Thomas, we recognize who he is because we have seen the print of the nails:

> 'Hath he marks to lead me to him
>   If he be my guide?
>   In his hands and feet are wound-prints
>   And his side.'

XXI

THE 'APPENDIX'

21.1-25

The Gospel of St John clearly ended at 20.31. Chapter 21 is obviously a postscript, and one which does not follow very smoothly upon the original book. Yet it explicitly refers to the Gospel (e.g. vv. 14 and 20) and seems to have been composed as an addendum to it. The stylistic evidence is ambiguous, since several typically Johannine words and phrases recur in it, while other quite new ones are also found. Thus, it is impossible to say with certainty that it is or that it is not written by the author of chapters one to twenty. Perhaps Chapter 21 was actually written in its present form by some disciples (cf. v. 24) who had often heard the author of 1-20 expounding these themes at the Sunday Eucharist at Ephesus; they added it as an appendix to his written Gospel. If this is in fact the true explanation, their addendum must have been included in the very earliest copies of the Gospel, as there is no manuscript evidence of its being a later addition. A difficult feature to explain is the leap from Jerusalem to Galilee. St John's Gospel had followed St Luke in locating the resurrection appearances of the Lord in or around Jerusalem, as against the tradition of St Mark (14.28; 16.17) and St Matthew (28.7, 10, 16) that they took place in Galilee; but doubtless this was necessitated by the character of the story of the Miraculous Draught of the Fishes. The story has obvious affinities with the narrative of Luke 5.1-11, but the latter is not a resurrection-story. Perhaps the best way to look at the story in 21.1-14 is to regard it as one of those pictures in which St John is using traditional material—in this case that of Luke 5.1-11—but is adapting it for his own teaching purpose. Our difficulties with the passage arise from treating it as an historical narrative designed to impart literal information about 'what happened'. As we have seen over and over again, St John is not concerned with historical details; he is presenting us with the truth of history in the form of a story. He is here teaching us the truth about the apostolic mission of the Church; and he is testifying to the presence and power of the Risen Lord, directing the work and feeding the workers with eucharistic food.

1. the sea of Tiberias
i.e. the Lake of Galilee; see 6.1.

2. . . . the sons of Zebedee, and two other of his disciples
Seven disciples were present, though it is difficult to find particular significance either in the number or in the composition of the group. The two 'Johannine' disciples, Thomas (see on 11.16) and Nathanael (see on 1.45), were there, and also the fishermen trio, Peter, James and John. There were also two unnamed disciples. According to v. 7 one of the seven was the Beloved Disciple, but his identity is tantalizingly undisclosed. He might be any of the group, except Peter whom he addresses. He might be the son of Zebedee or he might be one of the TWO OTHER OF HIS DISCIPLES. It is hard not to think that the writer is deliberately concealing his name for the very good reason that he was never an historical character at all.

3. Peter saith unto them, I go a fishing
Peter had returned to his home puzzled (Luke 24.12; John 20.10). Jesus was crucified, his mission a failure. Peter thought of becoming a fisherman again. But he could achieve nothing.

4. day was now breaking, Jesus stood on the beach

But all the time Jesus was not dead; he had risen at day-break, though his disciples did not know it.

5. Children, have ye aught to eat?

The Good Shepherd who feeds his flock stands ready to give his children their heavenly food, when they turn and acknowledge him; cf. Luke 24.35, HE WAS KNOWN OF THEM IN THE BREAKING OF THE BREAD. The expression CHILDREN (not used thus in John 1-20) reminds us of the LITTLE CHILDREN of I John 2.18, etc.

6. Obedience to the Lord's command brings not only success in the work but also the knowledge of the truth (cf. John 7.17). We know Jesus only when we obey his word.

7. It is the Lord

The primacy of the Beloved Disciple over St Peter in the matter of resurrection-faith is emphasized again (cf. 20.8). But it is the 'activist' Peter, the bold, natural leader, who takes the initiative in the Church's mission : it is he who first casts himself into the sea of the world and preaches the gospel to those outside (Acts 2.14; cf. Matt. 14.29). Nevertheless it is the 'OTHER DISCIPLES' (v. 8) who have to drag the net full of fishes, to cope with the multitudes coming into the Church (cf. Matt. 13.47, THE KINGDOM OF HEAVEN IS LIKE UNTO A NET, THAT WAS CAST INTO THE SEA, AND GATHERED OF EVERY KIND. . . .).

9. fish laid thereon, and bread

The meal is ready, before ever the disciples have offered anything from their catch. The significance of bread and fish in the early eucharistic symbolism of the Church must be borne in mind (see note on 6.11 above; the Feeding of the Five Thousand was also a meal of eucharistic significance by the Galilean Lake). See also v. 13 below.

11. a hundred and fifty and three

As Hoskyns remarks (p. 553), 'so long as the accuracy and supposed oddity of the number be explained as preserving the memory of the Evangelist who helped to count the fish, no true interpretation of the narrative as a whole is possible.' Clearly the number is symbolical. As every mathematician will see—and as ancient Greek mathematicians knew—it is a very interesting number; it is a triangular number $(1+2+3+4 \ldots +17=153)$ and it symbolizes perfection or wholeness. That is doubtless why (according to Jerome) ancient naturalists declared that there were 153 different species of fishes. The apostolic Church is engaged upon a world-wide mission, and the drag-net of the Kingdom of Heaven gathers OF EVERY KIND (Matt. 13.47), or, as the Johannine Apocalypse has it, A GREAT MULTITUDE . . . OUT OF EVERY NATION, OF ALL TRIBES AND PEOPLES AND TONGUES (Rev. 7.9). The number 144,000 in Rev. 7.4 is just such another number, representing wholeness, but the symbolism is drawn not from Greek natural history but from Jewish apocalyptic imagery.

the net was not rent

Contrast Luke 5.6, THEIR NETS WERE BREAKING. St Luke well knew the strain which mass conversions place upon the organization of the local churches; but St John has a different point in mind: in the Kingdom of the divine unity there is room for all mankind (cf. 14.2).

13. St John's allegory is breaking down because of the double symbolism of the fish. The disciples have brought their 'catch' (cf. Mark 1.17, I WILL MAKE YOU TO BECOME FISHERS OF MEN) to the eucharistic feast at which the Lord is host; but also the sign of the bread and fish, as in 6.11, is retained as a well-known eucharistic symbol. Bread and fish are frequently depicted in the representations of the Lord's Supper in the catacombs at Rome.

15. Simon, son of John
See note on 1.42 above.

lovest thou me more than these?
There seems to be no difference of meaning between
the two Greek words used for 'love' in vv. 13-17 (see RV
marg.). The threefold repetition of the question to Peter
is doubtless an allusion to Peter's threefold denial (13.38;
18.17, 25, 27). LOVEST THOU ME MORE THAN THESE?
probably means, 'Do you love me more than these other
disciples, as you said you did?' (John 14.37; Mark 14.29).

Feed my lambs
Cf. TEND MY SHEEP (v. 16), FEED MY SHEEP (v. 17).
There is probably no distinction of meaning among these
different forms. Christ is himself the Chief Shepherd of
the flock (cf. John 10.11-16; I Peter 5.4; Heb. 13.20; Rev.
7.17) and he now appoints St Peter as his principal shepherd ('pastor') in the Church on the earth. This is un-
doubtedly what St Peter in fact became. The pastoral office
of the 'clergy' (bishops and presbyters) was taken very
seriously in the Church in NT times (cf. Acts 20.28; I Peter
5.4; Jude 12). We must remember that in biblical symbolism a shepherd is a *ruler*, overseer (cf. Ezek. 34; Isa.
63.11), and God himself is the true Shepherd-Ruler of
Israel (Pss. 23; 80.1; Isa. 40.11; Zech. 11.7, etc.).

**18. when thou shalt be old, thou shalt stretch forth thy
hands**
The expression 'stretch forth the hands' means 'be
crucified'. A prophecy that St Peter would die a martyr's
death by crucifixion is here put into the mouth of Jesus;
v. 19 makes the matter quite explicit. Since it is virtually
certain that the 'prophecy' had been fulfilled by the time
that this chapter was written, we have here first class
historical evidence for the mode of the martyrdom of St

Peter—probably (as tradition says) in Rome (cf. Rev.
11.1-11, if the TWO WITNESSES are Peter and Paul, and if
THE GREAT CITY WHICH IS SPIRITUALLY CALLED SODOM AND
EGYPT is in fact Rome).

19. Cf. 12.33.

21. Lord, and what shall this man do?

The identity of ' THIS MAN ' is made very clear in v. 20;
he is the Beloved Disciple. And at the same time, in
typically Johannine fashion, his identity is very carefully
concealed. *Either* he is THE DISCIPLE WHO WROTE THESE
THINGS of v. 24, in which case he is a definite historical
character and an eye-witness of THESE THINGS, as v. 24
perhaps implies but does not quite say; *or* he is a symbolic
figure, not a particular person who can be named, but the
last surviving man who had actually seen the historical
Jesus. Probably the latter alternative is to be preferred,
because the death of the last surviving eye-witness raised
a problem for the Church: WHERE IS THE PROMISE OF HIS
COMING (*parousia*)? FOR, FROM THE DAY THAT THE FATHERS
(i.e. the apostles) FELL ASLEEP, ALL THINGS CONTINUE AS
THEY WERE FROM THE BEGINNING OF THE CREATION (II Peter
3.4).

23. This saying therefore went forth . . . that that disciple should not die

The Synoptic Gospels record a saying of the Lord which
was (wrongly) interpreted in some quarters to imply that
the *parousia* of Christ would take place before the last eye-
witnesses had died: THERE BE SOME HERE OF THEM THAT
STAND BY, WHICH SHALL IN NO WISE TASTE OF DEATH, TILL
THEY SEE THE KINGDOM OF GOD COME WITH POWER (Mark
9.1). St John is anxious to correct the view that Jesus had
predicted his return within the lifetime of the last living

eye-witness. The Lord had said that this was not a matter about which his followers should speculate (cf. Acts 1.7); their duty was to FOLLOW in the way of discipleship, even of martyrdom, whatever the date of his coming and whether the last eye-witness was alive or dead. WHAT IS THAT TO THEE? FOLLOW THOU ME.

24. This is the disciple which . . . wrote these things

Perhaps it is meant that the Fourth Gospel was written by the last surviving (so far as was known) eye-witness of the historical Jesus. We do not know. Nor do we know who are the men who add their testimony that his witness is true. The author of the Gospel, it would seem, has deliberately hidden his identity from us. It would help not at all if we could penetrate his incognito; his testimony would become neither more nor less credible if we could remove the veil with which he has hidden himself from us. It is not by the satisfaction of our historical curiosity that we are convinced of the truth of revelation, and St John has all along been concerned to shew us the inner truth of God's action in history for the sake of our salvation. He has refused to turn these sacred mysteries into 'problems' of historical research. When in faith we have received his testimony, and have learnt from him THAT JESUS IS THE CHRIST, THE SON OF GOD, we shall, from the depth of our inmost conviction, add our testimony to what he has written, and say, WE KNOW THAT HIS WITNESS IS TRUE.